Taking Flight *from* *the* Empty Nest

Mary Jenson

Harvest House Publishers
Eugene, Oregon 97402

Unless otherwise indicated, all Scripture quotations are taken from the New American Standard Bible®, © 1960, 1962, 1963, 1968, 1971, 1972, 1973, 1975, 1977 by The Lockman Foundation. Used by permission.

Verses marked NIV are taken from the Holy Bible: New International Version®. NIV®. Copyright © 1973, 1978, 1984 by the International Bible Society. Used by permission of Zondervan Publishing House. The "NIV" and "New International Version" trademarks are registered in the United States Patent and Trademark Office by International Bible Society.

Cover by Left Coast Design, Portland, Oregon

Published in association with the literary agency of Alive Communications, Inc., 7680 Goddard Street, Suite 200, Colorado Springs, CO 80920.

"The Road Not Taken" by Robert Frost is from THE POETRY OF ROBERT FROST edited by Edward Connery Lathem, ©1969 by Henry Holt and Co. Reprinted by permission of Henry Holt & Co., LLC.

"I Didn't," © Judith Gillis, 1998. Used by permission.

TAKING FLIGHT FROM THE EMPTY NEST
Copyright © 2001 by Mary Jenson
Published by Harvest House Publishers
Eugene, Oregon 97402

Library of Congress Cataloging-in-Publication Data

Jenson, Mary.
    Taking flight from the empty nest / Mary Jenson
        p. cm.
    ISBN 0-7369-0233-3
    1. Empty nesters—Psychology. 2. Middle aged women—Psychology. 3. Parent and adult child. 4. Family—Religious aspects—Christianity. I. Title.

HQ1059.4 .J46 2001
306.874'3—dc21   00-049852

Printed in the United States of America.

01 02 03 04 05 06 07 08 09 10 / BP-MS / 10 9 8 7 6 5 4 3 2 1

Acknowledgments

Thanks to Chip MacGregor, Carolyn McCready, and Terry Glaspey for encouraging me to write like I want to. And to Nancy Bayless and Jennie Gillespie, who kept my writing in line.

For Ron, Matt, and Molly—I love you more than my next breath. You have let me write about you in such detail that you may be the objects of many conversations over the years. You are brave and dear souls.

The father of the righteous will greatly rejoice, and he who begets a wise son [and daughter] will be glad in him. Let your father and your mother be glad, and let her rejoice who gave birth to you.
—PROVERBS 23:24-25

Contents

*My assumption is that the story of any one of us
is in some measure the story of us all.*
FREDERICK BUECHNER

Responding

Beginnings

There is no one home but me. It's June, early summer. Lunchtime. The children in the elementary school behind our house are shouting and playing on the field; not that long ago, it seems, Matt and Molly were among them. Though I have plenty to do, I'm longing for a diversion. Maybe a carpool run or something.

Maybe a last-minute dash to the store to pick up juice boxes for the kids' lunches. Maybe another science project.

Well, maybe not *that* kind of diversion, but, still, it's way too quiet here. Empty-nest quiet. I can hear the hum of the refrigerator all the way upstairs.

My nest isn't the only empty one. The first wave of baby boomer moms is hitting middle age, our children are flying the coop, and the world is watching to see how we're going to handle it.

Frankly, it's not the world's opinions that concern me. In my mind, the issue is much simpler. What will my life look like without my children to define it, and can I bear to let them go?

That's the question I'm working through for myself in this book, which is about a mother (me) and her children and the array of "leaving" experiences that assailed me as my children grew up. And it's also about reconnecting with my husband and reconciling with my age. For some time now, I've stepped back a little from my daily life and tried to be more of a spectator, determined not to miss any of the enormous transitions that I see happening in our family. That's not my natural inclination, even though I'm a writer and am supposed to be, by definition, *very* observant, itching to write down all my observations.

I'd rather stare out my window and think.

But I decided to think in writing because, now that my children are leaving, I know there are plenty of lessons the Lord has for me, and I don't want to forget them or have to learn them a second time. And I wanted to reflect because every bit of reflection helps to cement in my mind and memory the color of my children's hair, the sound of their voices, the touch of their skin. I love them! I'll miss the long talks Matt and I have when we can get them. I'll miss Molly coming in the room and flopping down on my *lap,* for heaven's sake. They are such a part of my happiness that there are fleeting moments when I wonder if I'll ever be happy again.

∽

Let me say from the outset that I've run the gamut of feelings when it comes to this time of life. When my kids were little I wanted time away and alone, to read, to sleep, to bathe without anyone wanting lunch. I asked for it for my birthday. Yet I loved my role as a stay-at-home mom; I did not have to put a career on hold, and, though I struggled off and on with my purpose in life, it didn't take more than a peek at their sweet faces to be satisfied again and again with where God put me.

When Matt and Molly (now in their twenties) entered high school, I began to explore the writing life. It seemed obvious that God knew I needed to find a vocation to fill my impending empty nest. And I was grateful. And relieved. And challenged. And, in a sense, ready for them to leave so I could get down to work.

But the closer my emancipation came, the more I dreaded it. My children were not merely projects that kept me busy, but likeable people, friends. All of a sudden, the thought of their leaving became more of a sentence than a reprieve.

And so there were days when I cried. Big, copious tears, full of pathos. Bittersweet sobs that arose from mind pictures of Matt preening in his Batman Underoos and Molly twirling in her ballerina skirt, her ponytails flying out around her like propellers.

And I cried not only because I wanted to keep building memories, but, frankly, because I felt scared and lost. This mothering thing was second nature, something I knew well. For twenty years they had been my "vocation." Soon, I would have to, in effect, change careers. And I was not interested anymore. Forget the writing. I wanted to keep my day job.

∽

Ron is my other half, the father of our two. This leaving stuff is hitting him hard as well. Though he's been a busy man all these years, he's made the three of us priorities in his life. He and Matt are best friends; Molly sits in his lap as well as mine. Ron and I have been married over thirty years, and I would say that a large part of what

I am—the largest part of the best of me—has come from his mentoring, from his modeling.

But there are changes in the wind for us. All our married lives we've been warned to pay attention to our relationship, for such a time as this—a time when the "distractions" have graduated and moved out and left us alone together. We knew it was coming, and we nearly ignored the warnings. Fortunately, this steady, good man I've married, who's missing our kids like I am and who has been patiently waiting in the wings, is still here and eager to grow with me as a couple. But it will take some work.

∽

Every morning in my quiet time I stumble all over myself thanking God for what He has given our family— closeness, undying love expressed in words and deeds, healthy relationships, little tragedy. I know it is His gift, not so much our doing, because there are plenty of parents out there who've loved their kids as much as we loved ours and are seeing rough times. I don't understand it; yet I am grateful that, as King David said in Psalm 16:6, "The lines have fallen to [us] in pleasant places."

And all along throughout the cathartic process of writing this book, I've wrestled with the fact that my story may not resonate with anyone else—at least, those who don't know me or my family. Yet as far as I can tell, my mother's heart is as fraught with many of the same anxieties as other mothers' hearts, my relationship with my husband—as one unique individual living in an empty house with another—requires the same kind of daily work yours does, my attempts at growing old gracefully are the same as any woman's.

So, here is our story. When the opportunity came to bring together all my observations in this book, to crystallize some of the lessons, I thought about the quiet I've waited for that is often too deafening, and about the last time the four of us sat around the dinner table together, and figured I'd say yes. It would happen anyway, this leaving, this change. It might as well be useful to someone else.

So come along, if you will, wherever you are in your journey with your kids, your husband, your hormones. I bet we'll have plenty in common by the end.

Hovering—
My Spiritual Gift

Hovering is my spiritual gift, my calling. I've determined this is so based on a quote by Frederick Buechner. "Your calling," he says, "is the place where your deepest joy and the world's greatest needs cross." Certainly it's clear that my children's world calls for watching over; and nothing could give me more joy than to be the presence in their lives that protects them from disappointment and need. They should recognize that it's handy to have a ready resource always at their side to spell difficult words, spot them some cash, or smooth down their cowlicks.

The problem is my children don't really like it.

They don't like it because they're in their twenties and ready to be out on their own. They don't like it because they're both quite self-sufficient in the important things of life and wanting to learn the things they don't know. And they don't like it because they know it's not healthy.

By the way, I know it's not healthy, too. Yet even that awareness does not motivate me to let go.

Hovering is the action of drawing in, of protecting, of gathering in, and it's part of our job as parents. Matt calls it hovering when I remind him he's late, or slow, or needs a haircut. For Molly, hovering is hanging onto her in public, and having too much to say in the fashion department. My friend Jennie didn't even realize she was hovering until her daughter, Jordan, stopped her on the stairs and accused her of following on her heels like a puppy.

Though we see hovering as protection, our kids grow to call it interference. It is not a lifelong "bullet" in our job description as parents; it's one that must be tabled at some point in their lives, regardless of our desire to reach out and touch them. When does hovering move from an essential to an interruption? Much sooner than we'd like to believe, I suspect.

I've read that something akin to a death must occur in the natural parent-child relationship, the death of one method of relating to make way for a new one. It's the kind of letting go that begins with weaning and builds with every new step of independence. So when we intervene time and again, refusing to allow our children to suffer the natural consequences (when we fill up their gas tanks, or wake them up in the morning day after day so they're not late, or continually hand them money when they're going out the door), we impede their independence, their growth. I found it hard to even type that sentence. I gave Molly twenty dollars the last time I saw her. She was short on cash and didn't want to have to go to the ATM. Tough love would have made her go anyway; healthy, non-hovering mother's love might have given her a lift, or at least required an IOU.

Recently Ron (a non-hovering dad) and I were feasting on fish tacos in a colorful little seafood restaurant. We were talking about our schedules, trying to anticipate our upcoming trips so we could balance our calendars. Matt would be leaving soon for the Philippines, and knowing that I would not be able to travel there with him as Ron gets to do, I mentioned that I'd like to go to visit him this summer.

"I don't think that's a good idea," Ron said. "It's not about you."

It took me a moment, but then I said, "Yes, it *is* about me. Matt won't need to see me as much as I'll need to see him."

"Okay," he said. "It *is* about you, but more importantly, you must put aside your needs and let him make his way there, get well established, even be lonely. He needs to know he can do this apart from us."

"Well, as long as you admit that it *is* about me…"

Once again, an opportunity to sacrifice for my child, to put aside the hovering instinct that needs to see where he lives.

Later that evening as I lay back in the bathtub looking at my tummy (still replete with stretch marks resembling dirt bike trails on treeless hills), thinking back on pregnancy and delivery, back on a little tow-headed boy very mature for his years, on a little girl slim as a stick with a penchant for flitting, I admitted my need to continue growing in maturity. I'll always want to intervene, to put forth my wisdom-of-the-years, to shoulder a burden that could otherwise make them stronger, better.

I realize now, in retrospect, that when we move out of our hovering role all we're really doing is changing the way we show our love to our kids.

And once again, this transition in our relationship rests on *my* shoulders. I'm the one who has to make the first move.

∽

I'm convinced, however, that hovering is a God-given instinct, necessary (for a long time in our children's lives) for the preservation of the species. It doesn't always reflect a lack of faith in God's ability or willingness to watch over our children. Rather, it's often a sign of the extreme interest in what's going on in their lives. A mother's need-to-know.

Jennie's daughter, Jordan, moved from San Diego to Seattle to attend Bible school and be out on her own. She found a job in a corner flower shop near Pike Street Market on the waterfront, an area of shops and produce, fish and flowers, restaurants and bookstores. Year round it teems with visitors and residents and has a flavor of excitement and interest about it. It also boasts several cameras situated on street corners, cameras linked to the city's website. A website that Jennie can pull up on her computer.

Once a day, in typical mom fashion, not to pry or spy but simply to know, Jennie logs on and takes a look around Jordan's corner. She can check up on the weather, on the traffic, on general Pike Street life. Though she's never seen Jordan—and they've tried to plan it so she could—it's all she really needs to know about Jordan's life. That little daily connection.

When Jennie told me this story, I laughed out loud, but I knew exactly why it was so important to her. I need to have a picture in my mind of *where* my children are and what their surroundings are like in order to be *comfortable* with where they are. There is something reassuring to a mother to know that, and often she doesn't *have* to know all that much more.

Surely, hovering is also one of God's attributes. We are to dwell "in the shelter of the Most High," and if we do we "will rest in the shadow of the Almighty" (Psalm 91:1 NIV). That sounds like the kind of hovering Presence we all need.

The Comfort of Home

❧

When I think about empty nests, my mind goes first to the day Matt started kindergarten, when he had to ride the bus for thirty minutes. He was the only child to board at his stop, and the first on the bus. Like any self-respecting mother, I followed that big yellow bus with tears streaming down my face all the way to the school, stunned by how small he looked and how mournful his gaze was out that window. I knew without seeing that his feet wouldn't be touching the floor, that he'd be holding his lunch box primly and properly and safely on his lap, and that he wouldn't move from his seat until told to do so.

(Remembering how my mother embarrassed me in junior high by bringing her knitting to Shadow-a-Student Day, I asked Matt on my first day of volunteering in his kindergarten class if he wanted me to wear or do anything special. He thought for a long moment, his eyes drifting to the ceiling, and then said, "No. Just be clean.")

Regardless of our personalities as mothers, even if we counted the hours until that first day of school when we'd suddenly be given the gift of time, sending our children into the world was, and still is, not easy. Each of us has stories of situations when our children made another tenuous step of independence.

18

When Matt was eleven years old, between fifth and sixth grades, we moved 100 miles south to San Diego. Is there ever a *good* time to switch schools and friends and neighborhoods and churches? Or rather, is change ever *easy*?

Matt would shake his head "No!" That summer he dealt with so many changes, inside and out. He and Ron and another son and dad spent a weekend going through James Dobson's tapes on *Preparing for Adolescence*. Rather than reassuring him, the tapes exposed Matt to things that hadn't even occurred to him. He spent some significant time that summer fearing the trouble he *could* get into, should he so choose.

Then we moved into the new house and to the new school, a private one fifteen minutes away by car. It didn't take long to recognize that the situation would be a challenge. His class teemed with difficult teenagers and was taught by a young, new teacher. Matt, who's disciplined and responsive to authority, felt things coming apart in the classroom from day one. The other kids teased him for doing his homework and *not* talking during class. They teased him on the playground for buttoning his shirt to the collar and not being rambunctious. When I picked him up in the afternoons, I found him angry and unhappy.

Years later, as I sat beside him one night as he drifted to sleep, he recalled his feelings so well. "Why isn't this bed as comfortable as when I was in the sixth grade?" he asked me. Then, before I could say anything, he answered his own question. In sixth grade, at this new school and in the new house, going through puberty, his self-esteem hit an all-time low. The only place and time he felt completely safe and comfortable was at home, in bed, asleep.

≈

That year, and the summer before it, marked the first time I really, really no longer had all the answers for Matt. Up until then I had been enough. I was his mother, for heaven's sake. I knew how to hold him, when to rub his back, how to draw out his thoughts. But that summer I knew I wasn't enough anymore. We sat on his bed one afternoon, where he cried, discouraged and frightened by the future. There, really for the first time—the first time we went out of *need*—we searched the Word of God together. We read psalm after psalm, hunting for the marvelous, comforting words of the Savior—not just the Savior of our souls, but the Savior of our daily lives, of our psyches. It was a powerful time. A teachable moment. Was this the real beginning of the letting go, when I realized I no longer had the power to comfort in the hardest of times and had to make the choice of transferring Matt's dependency to One who could?

Up, Up and Away

The many "leavings" of our children point to the frequent conflict between caution and risk taking. Do we pick them up in the middle of the night or let them cry? (Ron: "He needs to learn he can't control us." Mary: "But he's just a *baby*.") In our parenting, I'm the cautious one, and Ron's the risk taker. That's not uncommon. Usually Moms are more conscious of the consequences of actions, or maybe we're more likely to fear the worst than the best. Or maybe it's just me.

On one trip to Mexico with the kids, eleven-year-old Matt wanted to try parasailing, where one is strapped by a harness to a parachute and drawn out over the water by a speed boat and lifted high up in the air. Looking back, I can't believe I even allowed him to entertain the thought, much less let him do it! Yet I did, in a paradoxical moment of weakness and courage.

Ron approved of the idea, of course, and applauded Matt for wanting to try something so out of his ordinary experience. There seemed little I could do, and as Matt really wanted to, what could I say?

Men I did not know wrapped and strapped him into a parachute and explained with hand signals and broken

English (*now, what did they say, exactly?*) what to do, and then sent him on his way. He rose in the air like a puff of bubbles, light and quick and flimsy. His slight body allowed his parachute to soar higher than any of the others. I had my camera trained on him from start to finish, and I knew without a doubt that if I lost him in my lens I would never be able to pick him out of the sky, he seemed that small and that far away. With my eye pressed to the viewfinder, I whimpered like a feverish baby, shaking with quiet cries of fear. Ron alternately laughed and patted my shoulder, torn, I'm sure, between wanting to reassure me about Matt's safety and scold me for falling apart.

But I couldn't help it. It proved to be one of those moments when being in control was completely out of the realm of possibility. That, coupled with the potential danger, seemed more than I could bear. It was an extreme leaving moment.

∽

Come to think of it, parasailing is a very apt analogy for what we moms go through. At our children's insistence, we send them off into the world, where the language is different, where strangers make life-and-death decisions for them, where all we can do is catch a glimpse of them in the sky and whimper a bit.

His Children Will
Be Mighty in the Land

❦

$\mathcal{W}$hen the Lord speaks in a specific way, particularly through His Word, He makes it possible, even exciting, for me to let my kids move on to another stage of growth. God doesn't do that with me very often, but there have been several times where He's spoken so clearly that my only response, after obedience, is amazement. One of the most memorable times had to do with choosing schools.

After our little family moved to San Diego and had one nearly disastrous year in a private school, it became clear that we needed to do a little more research into the school situation. It fell to me to do the initial research, which I undertook with due diligence. I quizzed nearly every living, breathing parent I knew. You can imagine the answers I received. Each parent was as adamant about his or her opinion as the next. There was no consensus. I read books and magazines, studied the whole homeschool argument, visited countless schools—private, Christian, public, nearby, and faraway. All along Ron had been in favor of the neighborhood public schools, but I refused to make such an easy choice, at least until I'd done my homework. Finally one July morning as I sat on my balcony having my quiet time, I'd had enough ambiguity. I said to the Lord, "I've done everything I know how to do. I've had oceans of godly counsel. I've done the 'pro's and con's' list. I've been praying now since February. You've got to tell me *today* what to do this fall."

Immediately I sensed God saying to me, "Hasn't Ron said all along that you should put Matt and Molly in public school? So, do it! Follow his lead!"

It was an eye-opening moment.

Really, God? Follow his lead? Show me more.

Then I opened my Bible to the psalm for the day, Psalm 112. I read these words:

> Praise the LORD. Blessed is the man who fears the LORD, who finds great delight in his commands.
>
> His children will be mighty in the land; the generation of the upright will be blessed.
>
> Wealth and riches are in his house, and his righteousness endures forever.
>
> Even in darkness light dawns for the upright, for the gracious and compassionate and righteous man (NIV).

The words confirmed to me that public school would be a good place for our children. "His children will be mighty in the land." Even in the public schools, where a biblical worldview and Christian values are rarer than ever, there will be good influences and safety for our children.

The weight of decision making immediately lifted off my shoulders. Relieved, I first thanked God *profusely* for all the arrows He used to point me to His plan. Then I called Matt out to the patio and showed him what I'd learned. He agreed that there was no arguing with Scripture—and he was thrilled to be changing schools. Then I sheepishly went to Ron, admitted he'd been right from the beginning, and thanked him for his patience with my learning curve. That fall Ron and I put our children in public school, fully anticipating that, "Even in darkness light dawns for the upright."

Today Psalm 112 is written in calligraphy and framed above our doorway along with a picture of Matt and Molly as a reminder that God directs our paths.

The Comfort of Mom

olly has always been one of those children who wakes up smiling and doesn't seem fazed by life in general. She skipped a lot and sang and giggled as a child. Ron and I loved it, but it drove Matt absolutely crazy. Perhaps he felt life was just too serious to take so lightly.

But then came a period in her life when things didn't seem light at all and her joyful spirit suffered. It first showed itself when I'd drop her off Monday mornings at the kindergarten just down the street and she couldn't let go of me. I'd stick around as long as I could, and eventually she'd adjust to the day, ease into her role as student, warm up to her natural light-hearted personality. I took her unease as a clue, though, and homeschooled her (and Matt) for a couple of years. I'm so glad I did.

When Molly was in junior high, her struggles surfaced again. This time we gave it a name—separation anxiety. No more was it a Monday morning I-don't-want-to-go-to-school complaint. Rather, this monster grew fangs, and though everyday life was not much affected, things threatened to fall apart when Ron and I traveled and were not available to her. I think it stemmed from two things—her little body taking its own sweet time to come full swing into puberty (and thereby submitting her to all sorts of discomforts and health struggles) and the closeness we had developed over the years, particularly during these time of physical distress. For nearly three years, all the way into her sophomore year in high school, whenever we traveled we left a very unhappy child at home. Needless to say, I stuck around as much as possible.

So when Ron and I made plans to celebrate our twenty-fifth anniversary by driving through New England to see the fall leaves in October of 1994, I sent out a short but very specific prayer list for Molly to some of my closest friends. Once again, I knew I was not the answer for her. What I could tell her or say to her was not enough. Even the scriptures I wrote out in a little blank book for her to read when she felt worried were not enough. I called these few friends and asked them for specific kinds of prayers, from health to happiness.

Well, the separation, the feared anxiety, and the proof of God's love came together in those three weeks. She grew up an enormous amount, regained her happy countenance, and found her own inner strength with such assurance that I singled out in my Bible the words of Psalm 34:1-4 with this triumphant note, "When Molly's fears about our travel ceased!" David says in that psalm, "I will bless the LORD at all times; His praise shall continually be in my mouth. My soul shall make its boast in the LORD; the humble shall hear it and rejoice. O magnify the LORD with me, and let us exalt His name together. I sought the LORD, and He answered me, and delivered me from all my fears."

In my thank-you note to my praying friends I wrote, "Molly had peaceful day after peaceful day and handled each small emergency as well as we all knew she could. This was indeed a turning point in her maturity. She joins me in gratitude for your support and for God's answers."

Maple Syrup and Lobsters

✑

$\mathcal{L}$eaving for that twenty-fifth anniversary trip took a lot of mental preparation. Molly felt she needed me around, and I felt that as her mother that's exactly where I ought to be. Knowing the distress she might suffer kept me awake at night, even after I contacted my friends and asked them to pray.

Yet if an "empty nest" is to be as much a period, or evidence, of growth for me as it is for my children, I have to make steps of emancipation as well. Steps that show my children I'm not afraid of the separation, that I'm confident in their ability to stand on their own, that prove to *me* that I can do it, too. Steps that thrust me into new situations that will keep my life rich and changing. Steps that set my husband up for the attention he deserves.

As I vacillated between canceling the whole trip or running away with Ron without a backward glance, deep inside I recognized the importance of this getaway.

✑

Rather than tacking these two weeks onto another business trip, we intentionally set this time aside for us. We had a schedule only insofar as we made hotel reservations in advance for most of our nights away. We encountered the autumn weather we remembered from our childhoods, cold and windy, requiring warm coats and hats. We've missed that in Southern California.

One day we drove to Walden Pond, Henry Thoreau's getaway place, and dropped rocks on the rubble of his cabin along with many other pilgrims to solitude. We visited museums (Ron was so accommodating), chatted with Norman Rockwell's childhood models at one of them, and stopped at roadside stands for cider and fresh flowers. We reveled in the beauty of the leaves, the small towns, the quaint buildings, the enchanting cemeteries and public squares, the local heroes captured in stone.

Our favorite stop was Bar Harbor, Maine, which combined the extraordinary fall colors, the mountain hikes, and the coastline into one magnificent vista. Ron got his water; I got my trees.

∽

It shouldn't be such a struggle to recapture the sense of oneness in marriage, to find the romance again, to reestablish ourselves as a unit. But I felt the struggle, and I began to wonder, on this trip, just how far I'd drifted from my sweet husband, how much more stock I'd put in my mothering than in my "wife-ing."

Of course my concerns for Molly had something to do with my distraction, even with all the prayers I asked for and the nearly daily reports of her success. Still, I couldn't shake the image of my child, three thousand miles away, suffering in silence (or not) because we couldn't be with each other. I knew that Ron needed to be my priority on this trip, but my habit of hovering kept getting the best of me. Our phone bill proved it.

Ron and I talked about it a little on a hike in New Hampshire. I said that I'd been feeling a bit distant, not as appreciative of our time alone, not relishing it as much as I thought I would, not experiencing enough emotion.

He admitted to me that he hadn't noticed any distance, and I'm thinking, not "Phew! I got away with that one," but "Boy, do we have some work to do!"

It Was a Dark
and Stormy Night

*I*t *was* a dark and stormy night. Really. And on the heels of that disturbing period of separation anxiety I was looking at another separation I knew would test the lessons Molly and I said we'd learned.

In a moment of bravery and budding independence, Molly had made the decision to fly to Minneapolis by herself for a conference over the Christmas/New Year's break. Her friend Casey and her father would be at the airport in Minneapolis to meet her and would look after her for the several days she'd be gone. All seemed copasetic at the other end. Yet getting there was something else. I'm sure it felt safe back in October, after the major victory she'd won over her fears, but now as the dawn approached, we were both suffering.

As a mom, I can't help but be aware of the big bad world when it comes to my children. I take a mental note of every plane crash, every attack, and every kidnapping; and though I sympathize with the situation, I'm also relieved when I know where and how safe my children are. Even now that they're grown I still watch the news for plane crashes the day they leave for another part of the world. When I pray for my children, I begin with prayers of safety. It's instinct. It's so deeply ingrained in my every maternal cell I doubt I'll ever outgrow it. Though I don't talk about it in their presence anymore (I'm not *that* crazy), such thoughts are never far from my conscious mind.

So that night (Christmas 1994), when I awoke at 3:00 A.M., I foolishly allowed my maternal instincts free rein. At that hour of the morning I can jump to conclusions faster than anyone I know. And I did. First, I dwelt on the weather. The forecast confirmed substantial winter storms on her travel route from San Diego, through Denver, to Minneapolis/St. Paul. Opportunities for planes to ice up and go down, for long delays in airports, even the possibility for overnight stays in strange cities. How would Molly handle that at fourteen? What could I do and say that might prepare her for Plan B? That's the first concern that kept me awake.

Also, as a mom, I worry about my children when they're worried. If they're confident, so am I. I knew Molly was having second thoughts about this trip. She'd already had a few panicky moments the week before, shadows of previous hysteria, and it was all I could do to keep pumping her up and not let my own guard down. With her fears and tears came my own. That night it took an hour of silent suffering before I finally opened my Bible for some comfort.

I went to Psalm 91, a psalm of protection and a reminder that God's faithfulness will be our shield and rampart, our protection. As I prayed, I confessed that I actually wanted to trust the *weather*, for heaven's sake, and the pilot and the plane. And I even wanted to trust Molly, that she'd be able to rise to the occasion and pull this trip off.

Gently scolded with the sweet promises of that psalm, I felt better though I still worried. But then my eyes drifted across the page of my Bible to Psalm 95. "Do not harden your hearts," God said to me, "as [Israel did] in the wilderness….When your fathers tested me…though they had seen My work." What a rebuke! I sensed God saying, "You've prayed, you've seen Me protect this girl before. Stop testing Me! Keep praying, but quit worrying."

That was all I needed. And exactly what I needed. A reminder that God had never left me or Molly unattended before, and He never would. My job was to pray and thank Him…and rest. So I did.

When Molly woke up, she was definitely scared. Tears dripped on her knees as she sat on the edge of her bed. I knew just how she was feeling—and now I knew what to say. I sat beside her on her bed and gathered her into my arms, listening for a while as she sputtered out her fear. Then I showed her the two passages of Scripture I'd treasured during the night. She ate them up like sweet cinnamon buns, savoring all they promised and taking the rebuke to heart. By the time she got out of the shower she was singing.

She did look wistfully over her shoulder as she made her way down the jetway. I held back my emotions, too, but both of us had a new strength that morning. Yes, she made it to Minneapolis fine, no complications. And her three-hour layover in snowy Denver on the way home was cushioned by a new friend who was flying with her. NBD, as we say in our family. No big deal.

With all my lapses of memory, I am so grateful I can't forget that trip. That message directly from God the Father to His two daughters. Many times it has come to mind as I've sent her off on another adventure.

Psalm 95 is not a cure for hovering, but it certainly is a reminder that our God-given instinct to protect our children can go overboard. Certainly God puts us in place as moms, even gives us that drive to control and protect, but within that role, I think He has a better plan for our lives as well. A plan for peace and tranquility in the middle of the mothering. I like that.

Whose Socks Are Whose?

*C*ontrol is such an issue. In the large, big-picture sense, we have so little control over our lives. But in the nitty-gritty details, in the management of life, we moms exert tremendous control over our children. It's important that we do so, because rarely is there another adult in the household who *knows* whose socks are whose and which child will not eat beets regardless of the consequences. God gives us the ability to hold such details in our minds, and I believe He also holds us responsible for many other aspects of family life. It is not wrong for a mother to require information concerning the whereabouts of her children, or to insist on bicycle helmets, or to inspect little bodies for ticks and dirt. It is also not wrong for parents to invade a teenager's privacy if there is a reasonable suspicion of danger. God put us in their lives to protect them, to care for them, to raise them; from Him we get the authority to act, in many instances, in His stead.

But by building habit patterns of concern and control, all while our children are changing and growing in independence, we feed the mother-child monster that wants things to stay the same. Anytime you give your time and energy to someone else, your emotions become tied up, too. So we train them to leave us, not realizing that we need to be training ourselves in the leaving process as well. When others tell us lightly to "let them go," it's no wonder we want to laugh in their faces or shake our heads with that expression that says, "If you only knew what you're asking."

I look at it this way: Our goal and God's goal, if we're Christians, is to switch our children's dependence from us to Him. It's as if we need to go through their growing-up years intent on unplugging some of the many cords that connect us to our children and plugging them into God, or rather helping our kids do it.

In a very real sense, a healthy, independent human being is growing in dependence upon God. It's a paradox.

Releasing

The Launching

When I began dreading my empty nest—way before it happened, which is the manner in which I often go about things—I couldn't actually identify what concerned me so. Or rather, I could spout off an entire *list* of things I feared: a house that might become *too* quiet, children too far and "too much money" away, a change of job description, the loss of an accustomed identity (their *mother*), the challenge to a disciplined life without the kids' schedules to implement it. So many things.

Yet in the midst of all that angst, I appreciated the fact that we were nearing the launching, the sending off, the proving of our children. We were nearing the end of our responsibility for their character. And not only that, I hungered for even more discretionary time, and the freedom to take off at a moment's notice...or take a nap instead.

So when Matt began to look for colleges, I was ready. His leaving reminded me of another transition in his life, when he began driving. Though I'd worried about it, he had developed into such a responsible, trustworthy kid that the next stage in his maturity didn't faze me. (And though he will always be responsible and trustworthy, he didn't begin his driving career with flying colors...)

Matt wanted to go far away to the East Coast, to experience the Ivy Leagues, to live where the seasons change. He welcomed the idea of snow, of hallowed halls, of some sort of phantom college environment that would feed his philosophical, intellectual, introspective soul. (He's recently asked me to order this book for him: *The Reading and Preaching of the Scriptures in the Worship of the Christian Church: The Patristic Age*.) But as the Ivy Leagues weren't interested, UCLA and Wheaton College (in Chicago) became his choices. When he finally selected UCLA—two hours up the freeway—it wasn't hard to be happy. So much of happiness is related to perspective, and from my perspective, Los Angeles is a whole lot closer. That's what I cared about.

But here's what I wrote when he left, even knowing he'd be just up the freeway:

I walk by my son's room. No clothes on the floor, no comforter in a wad, no jazz on the stereo. I wonder, is an empty nest all it's touted to be? Have I been anticipating a quiet around here that I'm not going to like? I realize with a sinking feeling that periodically throughout their lives, I've been waiting to be rid of my children.

Far and Away

❧

$\mathcal{M}$y kids have been my excuses all these years. They have excused me from going places, from getting involved in others' lives, from expanding or escaping my comfort zone, from any kind of risk taking or courage testing. (One friend of mine said she's been living outside her comfort zone so much lately she's buying a condominium there. I'm not interested in joining her.)

So when Matt made the difficult decision to leave UCLA after his freshman year (so close and accessible, and I always knew pretty much what the weather was like) and transfer to Wheaton College in Chicago (too far away for my comfort), I decided I might just as well go see him and stretch myself in the process.

I flew alone (that wasn't new), rented a car alone (for the first time), found my way from O'Hare airport to the college alone (in the dark), and stayed in the hotel alone (and didn't talk to myself too much). Not a moment of anxiety or stress.

I lived through three seasons on that trip—summer in San Diego, fall the day I arrived in Chicago, and winter arriving the morning I left. I could tell right away the trees were straining to get this autumn show over and done with. Most still had their leaves; it had been so warm there hadn't been much inducement to turn, drop, and burn. But since I arrived, the mercury plummeted and things began to change. I drove slowly through neighborhoods looking down every street for the most brilliant performance. Don't get this kind of show in Southern California.

There was one—a tiny little sweet gum or maple (who knew from the road) that had turned the color of watermelon flesh. It even looked juicy.

Solo travel is not difficult for some people. (I kept reminding myself that I wasn't flying to some foreign country where they don't speak English or drive on the wrong side of the road.) But for me it represented a test, a risk. For two weeks I debated the car thing—should I rent one or get Matt to borrow one and pick me up? Finally I determined to grow. I have to take steps like this so that I don't implode with insecurities. (In my journal I wrote, *I'm taking a risk, Father, a risk with my habits but not a risk with You. Never a risk with You!*)

The day before I left I made a prayer list of all the things that were worrisome to me: having to switch to a different hotel because the familiar one where I wanted to stay—the one I knew how to get to—was too pricey this time, an assigned *middle* seat on the plane, landing after dark, and having to find my way alone.

And then in my journal I wrote from Chicago: *Jehovah-Jireh, God our Provider. Here I sit in the good, old, familiar Radisson in Wheaton ($1 cheaper than the unfamiliar hotel where I thought I'd have to stay!). I flew in a front window seat with no one in the middle beside me. I have a cute little white car, and I only made one teeny wrong turn on my way out here. (I did, however, bring the wrong shoes.) I'm* *having coffee in my room, by myself, and enjoying every minute. Lord, You are the Provider of Good Things.*

⁓

Wheaton College. I sit alone in the living room of Matt's on-campus house, taking in his environment, imagining him sitting on this couch or in that chair, napping on that floor, conscious of being the only woman here and so obviously a mother. What maternal undertones do I bring with me into this all-male house? Do I carry a scent of responsibility or judgment—or unconditional love—on my clothes? What other mothers do I represent, and is my presence here welcome by all five young men, or just by my own son? (And, is he *really* glad I'm here? Once I surprised him here on his birthday, and he didn't like it. He's a man who appreciates knowing what's coming and having time to prepare.)

Housemate Andy is in the dining room whipping up sheet cakes for student birthdays, looking for someone who will turn off the oven and take out his cake so he can pick up a friend after class on time. Other housemates are wandering in and out, up and down the stairs, preparing for other visitors, psyching up for the big football game. One of the seniors gives me a mum to wear—his "mum" couldn't be here for the Homecoming festivities.

I read the student newspaper, a collection of typical college meanderings but with a decided civility about them. One essay about the house next door filled with girls with a penchant for jigsaw puzzles, a report on the ongoing debate of "what to do" about chapel, a detailed full-pager on the "four steps to engagement by graduation."

I look around and take in the fish, the TV/VCR, Strauss waltzes on the stereo, mismatched furniture, several stacks of bedding for their constant overnight visitors, books crammed into the shelf with the gleanings of a Christian higher education, and the geriatric recliner the boys stole from the girls' house next door—in the middle of the night.

The house is surprisingly clean, although I find a few places to wipe up in the kitchen later as I'm drying dishes. I'm impressed.

Cleaning is not left to chance here. There's a "jobs chart" posted by the kitchen along with the prerequisite cleaning slogans: Whatever they use they replace or return; whatever they "dirty" they wash. Sounds like a song. And I get the distinct impression they did not clean the house just for me. Matt assures me he really does make his bed every single day.

I can hear two boys talking upstairs. Something about phone messages and then they move within better hearing range. This is what I hear: "So what do *you* use to clean the kitchen floor?"

I realize I've been given a rare gift—an actual interchange about *cleaning* between two college boys who don't realize I'm listening. For a mother, it's priceless. It's hope. It's a promise for the future.

That evening Matt and I are out on his porch, sunk in a soft sixties couch with gold plaid upholstery. It's early, still light, mild—about fifty degrees. The trees are red and gold, orange with a tinge of green. More leaves have fallen; I look for the crunchy ones to stomp in whenever we're walking. Tonight (it's Halloween) we're talking philosophy and handing out candy to the children who stop by. It's surreal—to be on *his* porch handing out candy to *his* neighbors.

I remember the year he dressed as a pirate with the black patch on one eye and the three-cornered hat. He wore a blouse of mine with puffy sleeves and a ruffly collar—as long as I swore not to tell. Those were bittersweet days, when he needed to try out what it meant to be a boy and I got to watch it happen. Not one for long talks then, nor for lap sitting or back stroking, he still always, always wanted me near.

Today at lunch we talked about the struggle between "working out our salvation with fear and trembling" and "cease striving and know that I am God." How the Christian world is exhorting us into this deep introspection about who we are and why we do what we do. What is our responsibility in the whole matter? We reached a temporary conclusion that too much preoccupation with how we relate to Christ ends up with our thinking too much about ourselves and too little about Him.

Rich discussion, good food, amazing company. I am proud of who he's becoming. I wonder what of me is in him. How did he turn out like this?

We walked out of the restaurant and he, from his position as the taller of the two of us, comments on my hair. "I like the gray," he says, although *I* don't think it's that noticeable. "It helps me move to the next developmental level."

Oh, brother.

On the Road Again

⁓

$\mathcal{M}$eanwhile, back at the house, Molly began making her own college preparations. That was a milestone in itself because, during her more anxious times, she'd actually asked me to identify the colleges closest to us. As I watched her explore her options, I secretly worried for her independence. In the end, her selection of Point Loma Nazarene University, a mere forty-five minutes down the freeway on a bluff overlooking the Pacific, was her first choice, not a default.

Amazingly, by God's sweet grace, Molly had come into her own. Her own strength, her own personality, her own sense of confidence, her own faith. It was beautiful to watch and required a celebration.

So the summer before she entered college, high in the sky returning to California from a wedding, we hatched a plan. Two hours after landing—and after checking in with Ron, who just happened to call home from his business trip and who loves spontaneity—the two of us left on a spur-of-the-moment car trip to Colorado.

It seemed like a crazy idea, a rash decision, a waste of time. But not long into our adventure, as I thought about Molly's departure for college in the fall, it seemed very important to take this trip, to do something impulsive, impetuous, that she would remember.

Our trip lasted six days. We put some healthy wear on my car, logged some significant time and dollars on the cell phone checking in with everyone, and implanted a grinning, gritty memory that I will never forget either.

On the road again. Up through California into the Mojave Desert, the wind hot, dry, and sandy blowing through the open windows. We were good at this—we macho women—our hair back in ponytails and baseball caps, riding high in my Explorer in our sleeveless shirts and jean shorts, barefoot in the heat.

We quickly found the desert radio stations, two of them that came through loud and clear regardless of the topography. We sang along to country western, contemporary rock, and oldies but goodies. Something for everyone. We swigged back our water bottles like cowboys do their canteens, rode with our elbows out the windows, mopped sweat from our necks with paper towels. We were something.

We wanted to make it to Colorado in two days. So we drove like the wind and didn't stop until midnight in a small town with a decent-looking hotel. Tempering the swagger, we exchanged our macho for femininity and found a nice room on the safer second floor where we slept like babies, exhausted and exhilarated.

Breakfast was from the grocery store: fresh-cut cantaloupe and a cereal snack pack we could eat with our fingers. The marketing took minutes and away we tore, across miles and miles of sandy ground, hills rising like hips and knees on a great flat beach. Promises of grandeur in the distance.

One afternoon, with hours of driving to go before we slept, Molly threw me a lure. "Is there anything about me you want to know, Mom?" It reminded me of the questions I'd asked my mother to keep her in the room at night scratching my back before sleep. It was a loaded question. Would I fire that gun? She was inviting me into some very personal territory and I knew it. I thought a moment and asked, "What are you afraid of?"

"Nothing," she answered quickly and decisively.

Not wanting to let her off so easily, nor to return to a more trivial subject, I reminded her of an earlier conversation about college—how she'd wondered whether she'd be capable of the work, how she'd feel living away from home. Yes, she finally conceded, there were some fears there.

"Of course," I followed, "that's natural. But you'll be surprised how you love it. Remember how scared you were when high school began, and how quickly you adjusted?"

And so another deep conversation, one complete with feelings and opinions and shared banter, began. Small, enclosed places at high speed, hour after hour, are ideal for lengthy self-revelation and the kinds of conversations that build relationships.

Emotional Food

It's never been hard for Molly and me to connect. Maybe her seeming need to spill her news the moment she had any is what made hovering so natural for me. She used to seek me out as soon as she'd walk in the front door and tell me, in detail, about everything and everyone that was part of her day at school. With that kind of regular emotional food (and I learned how to listen even when the tangents in her stories had tangents), we could talk about deep things and trivial. We would sometimes even go to the store together just to get some car time.

Then she took off for college, and daily contact and car trips became flings of the past. I no longer filled the role as her only confidante; she now had the undivided attention of her current roommates, who had their own stories to tell. She told them who sat with her at lunch, what happened in the parking lot, what cute boy asked her to dinner. And when we did talk, our conversation skipped the fun details of her life and, instead, dealt with necessary information or money.

What we're forced to give up as our children move on in their lives—to other "homes," to other people—is that never-ending storytelling. The small talk. The gentle arguments that help fashion our way of thinking. The immediate answers to the questions that pop up in unguarded moments. Is that what mothers lose when their children move away? Instant gratification?

What do I do with all I'm feeling, with the itch inside that is satisfied only in deep connection with my kids? What else on earth will be as fascinating to me as what's going on in their lives? Is it possible, is it even *right*, to wean myself away from all that intense interest?

It better be, I can hear my kids saying. For we are not open to being your only focus anymore.

And it dawns on me, again, like light sneaking through our vertical blinds, that the greatest change in our communication will come, not only as I adjust to my kids' new place, but as I adjust to *my* new place. It's not just letting them move on; it's making my own commitment to move and change. Once again, it's their growth that prods my own.

Worldly Goods

It's winter and my house is full of people who like each other. Matt and Molly are home for the holidays from their respective schools, we're housing dads and moms, big kids, little kids, a good old dog, and two pet snails. Productivity is down because communication is up. We all love it.

Somehow, with nary a blink and but a weekend in between, Ron and I went from a brand-new empty nest to Hotel San Diego. There were fewer echoes than I expected from the children's rooms, no lonely basketballs or quiet pianos, no clean, bare cupboards, no orderly refrigerators. Off to college went the two Jenson kids, and in moved Dave and Lisa Everitt, along with Malachi (seven) and Mary (five). For a year.

Once again we have refrigerator art, waist-high fingerprints on the sliding glass doors, and snippets of art projects dotting the carpet like a mosaic. We *love* this family. We've missed the way kids fling themselves at you when you walk in the door, we've missed the thuds of kids romping in the bedroom above or jumping down the last of the stairs, we've missed little squeaky pink bodies (*kid* bodies) fresh and fragrant from the bath.

People's mouths drop open when they hear we had an entire family of four live with us for a year. We, too, find it hard to believe. Particularly me.

∞

There is no hard and fast rule that says an empty nest has to stay that way. As nature abhors a vacuum, so it should be that our empty houses, our empty arms, look for ways to be filled. I guarantee you, though, that Ron and I weren't looking for other people to fill up our newly vacant bedrooms. But when the need arose, it simply made sense. When we're at this stage in our lives, I don't think God wants us retreating to our bedrooms, refusing to take calls from anyone whose last name is not the same as ours.

Our need for community doesn't diminish when our built-in community disperses. It merely takes on a different complexion. We'll always need to connect with others. That's why we tell stories, why we write letters, why we go to movies with friends and meet for coffee at a moment's notice. It's why we struggle to get our pictures in albums and send out Christmas cards and ask for everyone's e-mail address. It's why I call Ron to the backdoor to see the sunrise, and why I point out to every visitor the hummingbird nest in our creeping fig. We were made to share those things, to share ourselves, to connect with a community.

With our children around, a community in themselves, I could be selective about outside relationships. They were a wonderful excuse to keep us secluded. But now that our "excuses" are beginning to move out, leaving empty bedrooms, it's our new challenge to be aware and inviting of the concept of Christian community in its broader definition. God seems to have a plan to bring other relationships into our lives.

∞

Dave and Lisa worked with our kids' youth group some years ago, stayed with our kids now and then when we traveled, took them camping and rock climbing and hosted rubber band wars in the living room. (I still find occasional evidence of those wars in the book shelves...) They became adept at kid-speak, although they weren't that far removed from it themselves. Dave's passion and concern and Lisa's passion and wacky humor became a fortress of sorts for many kids around us.

Then, joining Church Resource Ministry's outreach to the poorest of the poor in Cambodia, they went with their tiny children to live as the least live in that war-torn country where land mines create killing fields all over again. But they called it "Paradise" and reveled in the fresh fruit, the fresh fish, and the fresh hearts that were so open to the Good News.

When the time came for a little R&R, necessary because of Dave's battle with dengue fever, they looked for a harbor—a community, a home with a few people around to be a part of their lives. They needed a little healing, a place where there could be interactions with other adults who cared. They asked about moving in for a time, and it sounded like a good idea to us—in fact, each one in our family, when I questioned him or her, answered, "Cool." It was our turn to be the fortress.

We had our share of adjustments, involving belongings, space, food—we drank different kinds of milk, ate different bread, couldn't come to any conclusions on the butter versus margarine debate. We shared deep conversations with Dave and Lisa—and movies and ice cream. The children wrestled with us, coerced us into playing basketball and Monopoly, snuggled with us in front of the TV or at night before bed. We built a bond as strong as family. We became family.

Malachi and Mary didn't erase the emptiness that Matt's and Molly's leaving had created—who can take the place of your own children? But all the activity, the bath toys, the noise, and the singing filled up our home and gave us the feeling that we were doing just what the Lord wanted us to do.

∽

May 1998. Both our kids have come home from college bringing back all their worldly goods; the Everitts are still here with all their worldly goods; and Ron and I, of course, have all our worldly goods here as well. It occurs to me that the people fit fine in our house; it's all their worldly goods that are driving me crazy.

∽

October 2000. Is there a greater gift than knowing you've made an impact on another life? Can a family be more blessed than hearing how that impact continues to make a mark in the world? In total humility and awe I read this latest e-mail from Dave:

> We recently had a family meeting to consider inviting Rith's wife Rachina and their one-year-old daughter to live with us. Lisa and I laid out what we considered the costs and benefits of inviting them to live with us. Then we asked Mac and Mary to be open and tell us what they really thought

before we made a decision. Mary said, "Don't you remember how Uncle Ron and Aunt Mary opened their house and family to us? They became like blood to us. Like in the *Christie* movie where the girl said, 'Family is not just who you are born from, it's a matter of *who* you choose to care for.' We need to be like Uncle Ron and Aunt Mary and bring Rachina and Bopha into our family."

Thank you not only for the blessings of being with you, but also for the love embossed on the hearts of my children. We remember how you cared for us, how you laughed and cried with us, and how you prayed for us. We are happy results, or at least works in progress, of your love and ministry, and we deeply miss you.

Worldly goods are no match for the lives and personalities they represent. What's a little chaos when the love is strong?

Laying the Easter Egg

ﾟﾟ

With our kids coming and going as young adults now, we're moving into some new ways of relating. Take the previous Easter for instance.

Dark rain clouds that spilled over into our gardens the previous week had been displaced by fluffs of white clouds in a robin's-egg-blue sky. Our church was packed, people elbow to elbow, worship and praise filling our cavernous sanctuary like the incense which filled the temple long ago. Surrounded by immediate and extended family, I felt like a hen with a nest full.

Later, Ron, Matt, Molly, and I joined our good friends and their family for dinner. One couple sitting there, balancing dinner on their laps, had led worship that morning. Molly told me they might have advice for her, seeing as she senses God is calling her to a similar ministry. Of course, I said.

Linking her arm through mine, I walked up to them, not strangers to me, and introduced Molly. She was gracious, as were they, and wanting to help along the cause, I said to Molly in their hearing, "You can carry on the conversation." I walked away, confident I'd started the ball rolling, but something compelled me to look back. Molly had disappeared.

I made the rounds visiting with friends and acquaintances, introducing myself now and then, ending up in the food line hungry for the scalloped potatoes and that rice thing with the green chilies that Kristen makes. Every few seconds I looked around for Molly's red sweater. She shouldn't have been so hard to spot in this sea of Easter pastels.

So when my plate was clear, I headed for the food line again—but really I was looking for my girl. Upstairs the boys hovered around the pool table like patrons at a cockfight, the bedrooms were empty (at least of girls in red sweaters), the living room and family room had none of my family in them. Back outside I joined an in-progress conversation, knowing deep inside Molly was gone because of me.

Finally, I saw her coming around the side of the house—couldn't miss that red sweater—and I went to intercept her in the kitchen. She'd gone on a walk. By herself. She waited till the room cleared and confronted me up against the oven; my back was warmed with the afternoon's baking.

"You embarrass me," she said—and the old issue surfaced, alive and kicking. The familiar *faux pas* I'm so often guilty of—controlling too many details of her life. Forcing her to connect with people when she wants to make her own way. Guiding her too obviously, too hen-like, clucking and shooing and hovering. Doesn't take much from my mouth for my grown children to feel like little kids again. I wish I could have remembered sooner how she felt (because we've been through this before), and I wish I could have sucked those words back in my mouth like you suck a thick strawberry smoothie up a straw.

Molly was right about what she said, and I deserved every word, and she treated me kindly yet firmly as she talked to me. I think this is called "speaking the truth in love."

Speaking the Truth
in Love...Again

Not long after the Easter "incident," Molly and I hit the mall. She's normally a thrift-store shopper, looking like a million bucks but spending only five. However, now and then we go to the mall to shop together—she loves having me come because I usually pay. One such day, as we were looking through the various displays and racks of clothes, I could feel her becoming more and more distant. Finally she said, "I don't want to be here. Let's go home."

Obviously something was bugging her, and I thought it might be the zit on her forehead. But when we walked out of the store and stood there in the center of the mall she told me the real problem. I was touching her too often, suggesting she try on things that she really hated, playing the mother bit too much.

Hovering once again.

In a wonderful moment of mother-lucidity and sacrifice, I handled it well, congratulated her for being open and forthright, apologized for intruding too much, and offered to go do my own shopping and meet her for lunch in the food court. She brightened like one of those flowers that opens in the sun. It was a small moment, seemingly insignificant in terms of time and space, yet it further established a safety zone for us. She confirmed that I can take what she has to say, if she's kind; I learned once again that it's possible to handle with grace the inevitable confrontations that come with living together.

If I am to embrace the independence and health of my adult children, I must also submit to their "take" on my personality, on my strengths and weaknesses. It's the way it should be. They probably know me better than anyone else; it's how I act at home that gives away my true character.

That's what makes me want to celebrate situations like Easter when Molly let me have it right in the...control center. I *love* it that she's brave enough and confident enough, in herself and in me, to confront me. I love it that she cares enough about our relationship to do something proactive about it. And that she's careful to couch her words in love. She breaks down my defenses and makes me want to be a better mother, and, therefore, a better woman. And she increases my assurance that she will be ready to be on her own in that big, bad world out there.

And I continue to be ripe for confrontation. Not long ago I hovered once more and embarrassed myself and Molly in front of her friends. I didn't notice the awkward silence at first (I can be so dense sometimes). For a while I felt frumpy, old, and in the way. But Molly and I talked, and after I'd apologized, I helped her to see that hovering is instinctive and now and then appropriate for a mom. And she called me "teachable," which made me smile because I was thinking the same about her.

Micro-Body

~

$\mathcal{I}$'m intrigued by the concept that our little family, grown up and spread out, is the body of Christ in miniature. It's Ephesians 4:15 in action, "Speaking the truth in love, we are to grow up in all aspects…." Our families are constructed, by God Himself, to *make* us grow up. That's why we're married to the person we're married to, and why we have those squirrelly children God gave us. There has been no mistake. Our children are His gifts to us, not just for our pleasure and responsibility, but also, specifically and pointedly, for our growth and maturity. Scary, isn't it.

My older and wiser friend Nancy and I talk about this now and then—how mothers relate to their children and how, though the ages and stages change, our kids will always be instrumental, knowingly or not, in our growth. Just recently she traveled overseas with her two children and their families and ended up having to apologize for her attitude by the time they parted. And she's seventy-six. I guess it never ends.

Now that Matt and Molly are in their twenties, whether they're underfoot or not, the focus on and of the Word of God has radically changed for us as parents. Gone are the "spare the rod" words and in their place are the "one another's," the verses that apply to our relationships with…one another. Although our children will always be our *children*, they eventually become that "one another" person the New Testament talks about with such regularity (Galatians 5:13; 1 Thessalonians 5:11; Hebrews 10:24; 1 Peter 5:5). That's where we're camping now.

If Ron's and my relationships with Matt and Molly are to continue to grow, continue to be meaningful, they have to move from the parent-child bond to the more reciprocal connection of friends and fellow-members of the body of Christ.

And *that* means we have to be ready to receive the criticism, to hear the counsel, and even to seek these things from our children. Kids usually take whatever chances they get to correct their parents. Now that they are grown up, because it's healthy and right and mature, we moms and dads with grown kids should ask for it.

Bearing Burdens

As we move from parenting to friendship, it may not seem like much of a stretch for a mother to focus on passages such as Galatians 6:2, "Bear one another's burdens, and thus fulfill the law of Christ." Haven't we been doing just that all these years, bearing burdens?

Yet that's what I think the parenting message of the new millennium is for me: Learning how to bear my children's burdens in a different sense…and assuming as well that they will help bear mine.

First of all, I want to be careful to acknowledge all that might be going on in the minds and hearts of my children as they prepare to leave home for good. Over the years we have prayed both huge and minuscule prayers, just like every family that believes in prayer. But now they are making life-changing and lifelong decisions about education, jobs, and spouses. Perhaps, along the way, I felt as weighted down with some of my kids' needs as I do now. It's possible. The difference lies in the fact that I cannot hover anymore. Though my counsel might be requested, the decisions are all theirs.

Second, now as I pray for their spouses, I recognize I need to pray that they'll find mates who will take over the burden bearing. That's all part of the "leave and cleave" command in Genesis. It's a good thing to look for in a husband or wife, I will tell our kids—someone who will bear their current burdens with love and patience and who will promise to go on doing it for the rest of their lives. (I might even encourage them to spell those burdens out, anticipate the kinds of things that could weigh on them, and their spouses, in the future.)

And I will learn to resist the temptation to continue on in my exalted position as *chief* of the burden bearers. Oh, I'll still pray. But once they're married, the spouse takes over—unless I'm asked.

(Vicki's daughter married a wonderful guy last summer. Shawn loves Annie with his whole heart. Not long ago she had her wisdom teeth pulled, and awoke after her surgery in a drugged stupor. Poor Shawn had never seen her like that, had never seen *anyone* like that. Next thing Vicki knew, he appeared at her door with Annie in his arms and panic on his face, looking for some burden-bearing help. And Vicki gladly gave it.)

Third, I will also now admit that burden bearing is a two-way street.

The burden-bearing passages (for example, Galatians 6:2; Romans 15:1) are for "one another." They mean, now that we are all adults here, I can be honest and forthcoming about *my* weaknesses and struggles. That I *should* ask for our children's involvement in praying for me and my concerns, just as I am involved in praying for them.

This is an important transition for me. All along I've also been their shield, knowing they didn't need to understand all the particulars of life around them. Now, if I am to let them go, if I am to loose the familial hold, if I am to cut those apron strings, I must welcome them into this inner circle of truth, faith, and relationship. It's a paradox: I cut the ties and welcome them to a new place, to the even stronger cord of mutual responsibility. It's what a family of adults does…puts away the past and enters into a different and new sort of relationship.

Yea! I need all the prayer I can get! I *love* it that our children want to pray for me, want to know what gets me down the most, and care about my spirit. After all, I've been caring about theirs for so long. It's only right.

⁓

So last year I had a bit of a scare, a thickening under my arm that caused my doctor to send me immediately for a chest X ray and a mammogram, then a meeting with the surgeon. It hit me hard. I walked around Costco with my thoughts way, way offtrack, so absentminded I missed the vendors with the sample goodies they're all too willing to share with me.

Though I'd been able to talk to Ron on the phone, he was out of town, so Matt took over as the man of the house. That night we went out to dinner, and I told him everything (but not exactly *all* that had been on my mind as I walked the Costco aisles). Then, after a soft admonition from my son about my holding out on him throughout all these appointments, we bowed our heads, and he prayed such a prayer! He blessed me with his insight, his compassion, his steadiness, his faith. He gave me confidence in God and in him, that *both* of them would be able to carry out their parts in this predicament. It's an awesome thing to be prayed for so completely by one's child.

And nothing at all came of that concern and aimless walking. Thankfully.

Then this year, another breast cancer scare. An obvious "something" on the mammogram, same breast. Now I did not wait to share with our children. Rather, I wanted as much prayer as I could get as early on as possible. The ultrasound showed a cyst plain as day. No concern, no action taken. We all rejoiced...because we'd all been praying.

This past Christmas, the four of us shared three major prayer requests we had for the coming year, requests that addressed deep needs and the issues we struggle with. In only a month we saw some *major* breakthroughs. The most important way to begin bearing burdens is to tackle the hard stuff and watch to see what God will do.

Our children have always played a major part in our growth. But no more is it a passive lesson, "teaching" us by their mere presence to be more patient or more loving. Now it is in terms of partaking in the nitty-gritty of our lives. They are rolling up their sleeves and joining us in the race for righteousness. We're all four running it together, arms linked, heels clicking.

Great Expectations

All these years I've been torn between wanting my kids to stick around for life and wanting them to take off so I can *have* a life. With Ron. I am not the only baby boomer woman trying to reawaken my old love with my husband, now that there's time for it. However, I'm surprised it's such a struggle.

After a summer of heavy commitments, a good friend of mine and her husband took off on a two-week, second-honeymoon-like vacation. Unfortunately, they weren't seated together on their over-full flight and were stuck on the tarmac for quite a while. The flight was long and not once did this husband check on his wife. And when she walked by his seat to say, "hi, I love you," he seemed perturbed, disturbed by the interruption. She realized it was only because he'd lost his train of thought; that he's a good man, a kind husband. Yet she was hurt as she recognized his slim understanding of her need for connection now that their children are gone.

Now that *our* children are gone more and more, Ron and I are learning how to vacation again, and how to do it together, alone. Being such independent souls, it's quite a bit of work. And I'm trying to figure out why.

This time, Ron and I are taking a few days of R&R between obligations. He says this is our first mini-vacation of several this year. At the airport we jockeyed for the best possible legroom situation, either an exit row or two seats with an empty one between, or maybe even an upgrade. I'm thinking, at the time, how much we like to be in control of our environment, smugly glad Ron is so proficient at landing us good seats, getting us a good deal. We find our spots in the roomy first class, a nice perk his frequent travel affords. I settle into the smooth, gray leather seat, stretch out my legs and flex my feet, tired from the scurrying to get there on time.

Behind us at the bulkhead is a mother with her baby and all the accompanying paraphernalia. Without being able to see her I know exactly what she's doing: figuring out how to get her baby comfortable, wondering where to stash the diaper bag (seeing as she has no "under the seat in front of you" to use), praying that the middle seat stays empty. Her pockets and purse are stuffed with crackers, juice, small books, crayons, and pads of paper—and maybe some motion-sickness medicine for sedation purposes. She's carrying tissues, diapers, wipes, bottles, pacifiers, blankets, extra T-shirts and overalls, and the favorite soft toy which is the only thing that will ensure her child's emotional comfort. Been there, done that.

The young mother and I smiled when she passed, that smile that says it's tough but well worth it, that says I know what you're going through, this too shall pass.

I don't miss the traveling part of having children. Even without them, it's going to be a long day of flying. And I can tell Ron has a lot on his mind; I know he has several deadlines looming over his head. Or rather several deadlines that would loom over my head but merely energize this man so different from me. He is arranging his lair, putting his coat overhead and grabbing a pillow for his lower back, hoarding several computer magazines from the plane's stash in the seat pocket in front of him, unpacking his own collection of magazines to go through on the trip, and pulling out a file of work I can barely fathom.

I wrap myself up in a flimsy airline blanket in the window seat and pull out a book for the beginning of the flight. I'm a little sleepy, but hoping we can do some talking.

So I read for a while and am conscious of being close to the man I love. Yet for the next six hours our only conversation relates to food and schedules, despite the plea I'd made at the onset that I wanted to talk about a few things. I realize I'm encroaching on his domain. For a long, long time he's traveled alone. He's learned to use every moment of travel time for something constructive, even if that means a good, hard nap.

But now I'm along. I have these expectations, you know. I expect that when he says he wants me along, he means he wants to be with me in every sense of the word. I expect him to make great use of our flights to grow closer in soul and spirit, to have long, searching conversations that reawaken us as to why we fell in love in the first place. However, it's not that easy, and it's not yet that way.

Altars and Nose Rings

While Ron and I began exploring this new stage in our lives, our kids racked up more time and bills at Wheaton and Point Loma Nazarene. In both cases I'd *been* there, seen their rooms, met their roommates, and walked their campuses. I was settled with their settling, content with their choices, and not worried about their future.

Then Molly made plans to go to Bulgaria on a missions trip with other kids from school. Ron couldn't suppress his excitement that Molly would be stretched in this significant way. I scoured the Internet for reports on infectious diseases and inoculations.

Sitting there on Molly's college bed early in the evening before she left for Bulgaria, looking out on the bluest ocean and the blue-white hazy sky (who wouldn't want to go to school here?), I noticed several strands of her hair, long, blond, tangled, in the sunbeams resting on her sweatshirt. That evening Molly came across as long, blond, and slightly tangled herself.

Earlier on the freeway, as we confronted her anxiety about her trip, we talked about courage and rising to the occasion. How she has grown to emerge as a leader when one is called for, how she's been fearful in the past, yet when the feared situation actually comes upon her she's now more than up to the challenge. Macho woman.

That evening my child needed my encouragement as much as ever. Words had to come that would build her up, remind her of past strengths, give her courage in the moment and for the journey. I recalled for her what we both had learned that Christmas so many years ago. *Keep praying*, God had said, *but do not test Me. I am able. I am capable and loving and I will not let either of you down. Ever.*

Of course bringing up those verses and that lesson comforted me as well, not only for that moment, but the whole time she was away. Talk about being out of the loop. In the middle of her adventure, I went way beyond wondering how she was eating, to wondering if anything (like maybe a parasite) was eating her. I found myself so out of control it made me laugh. Or maybe it painted a clearer picture of how out of control I am of her life anyway. Here or there. Then or now. And probably that's exactly as it should be.

Molly and her team had a wonderful experience in Bulgaria—three weeks of hard, physical work (building washing shelters for Gypsy women), plenty of ministry opportunities (including Molly's preaching what she termed her first—her *first?*—sermon), and they grew to love one another (but no *one* in particular). It was all we'd hoped for. The details spilled out over the ensuing days and weeks. Molly's account of drinking the water and running barefoot through the village appalled me. Yet I loved the pictures of her sitting with her guitar, surrounded by the little village children.

She e-mailed once from across the world: DEAR MOM. I'M HERE, I'M SAFE, I'M HEALTHY, AND I LOVE YOU. LOVE, MOLS. Though I wanted more, lots more, she told me all I really needed to know.

The big night of the team's homecoming finally came. Ron, Matt, and I made it to the airport with just minutes to spare. They straggled off the plane, tired and smiley, to the balloons and hurrahs of family and friends who couldn't wait to hear their stories. I remained completely under control, however. Then came Molly. With a nose ring. And I cried.

As I buried my head in her sweaty little neck, determined to ignore the jewelry and concentrate on the child, I knew deep in my heart her safe homecoming meant so much more to me. So, smiling, I pulled away and held her at arm's length, taking in the rest of her, when a sly, wicked grin began to play about her lips. She reached up to her nose and pulled off the silver hoop. It was a fake.

∽

The same day I sent Molly off to Bulgaria, I joined many others in the final send-off of Beth's two-year-old Michelle, who died after a ten-month bout with cancer. It was heartbreaking.

Is there any similarity between the temporary loneliness I feel with Matt and Molly gone off to Bulgaria, or college, or the rest of their lives, and Beth's deep, penetrating, lasting loneliness? Between my fears and Beth's agony? Between my empty nest and hers?

There is no comparison.

Yet, is God not with both of us, sovereign in both cases, and intimately involved in all the details of our lives? We know He is all-good and He makes no mistakes, nor does He act capriciously. Why is that knowledge—and I believe it with my whole heart—sometimes of such little comfort?

Protective Clothing?

Matt had his own Eastern European missions experience, planting a church in Moldova with a team from a church near us. He walked through villages, knocking on door after door, introducing the plans for the new church and sharing the gospel.

Somehow, probably because he's a guy, the oldest, mature beyond his years—and because I knew the leaders—this trip didn't hit me with the same intensity as Molly's.

But then he flew to Europe with a friend, on a shoestring budget for three weeks one summer, spending the first week by himself in France, trying out his French, living in hostels and with friends, and meeting up with his traveling buddy in Nice. It unsettled me that he'd be traveling alone for a while. I have a firm conviction that two are better—and safer—than one.

The night he left, he asked me to buzz his head so he wouldn't have to deal with his thick hair. I'm not good at cutting hair; even when he was little I did the bare minimum—and then usually had to take him quickly to the barber. I warned him as I assembled the big shaver that his good looks (maybe even his life) were in jeopardy. But determined to get his buzz, he found himself stuck with the "barber" at hand.

Not in a long, long time had I felt such closeness with him. He's a man now and rarely invites me to comment on his grooming, much less participate in it. But as I stood above his chair and guided the hair clippers over his skull, I felt a physical connection with him that surprised me. I'm sure he had no idea of my feelings.

Then off he went; glad to get out of the house I'm sure, glad to be on his own in every sense of the word. And I went inside and cried.

Don't get me wrong. It thrilled me that he had such an opportunity (and that he paid for it out of his own pocket). I trust him, and God, and I had no irrational fears for his safety (which didn't mean I neglected to pray for him often). But those particular three weeks Ron was also out of town, and Molly had left for her summer camp counseling job. All the "alone time" I'd been waiting for had materialized, and I realized that, because it was no longer my choice, I didn't like it. I had way too much time on my hands not to worry.

Then, the week after Matt's return from Europe, a group of summer holiday travelers lost their lives on a river in Switzerland. The name of the sport, "canyoning," had a familiar ring to it. I asked Matt about it. "Oh yeah," he said. "I know what that is."

Then I showed him the article in my magazine, and he told me he slid down the same river, in the same Swiss canyon, with the same organization, in the same "protective clothing," two weeks before. I nearly fainted. I am *so* glad I find these things out after the fact.

When I give serious thought to the faraway places my children have traveled, and to the danger Matt encountered, I wonder how moms send their children off when they *know* their lives are threatened—children who go to war, who make heroic choices to serve others in difficult locations, who make *poor* choices to live dangerously.

Is God enough when our kids are in tight spots or rebel? Is He capable of handling them in danger, in their disobedience—and us in our fear—at the same time? We know He is, but sometimes I wonder how Barbara does it, whose two sons go wherever the Army sends them. And how Maggie does it, whose eighteen-year-old daughter left home to live with her boyfriend.

This hand-off stuff—really, finally, totally handing your children off to God and the world—is much harder than anyone told me it would be. It takes practice I think, but the practice sessions we're given are not anywhere near adequate enough. Rather, it seems, they leave, slam bang…and moms just have to deal with it.

The Road Less Traveled

℘

Not only do we have to deal with the adventures our children pursue, the dangerous things that would make us whimper if we knew about them beforehand, but we also have to be ready, often at the drop of a hat, for the detours they take from "the plan."

On Christmas Eve day 1998, our little family of four sat enjoying a wonderful lunch at the Plaza Hotel in Manhattan. Outside, the sky was the color of silverware and the wind just as cold and unforgiving to the touch. But inside, surrounded by dark, paneled walls, we luxuriated in deep leather chairs and dipped heavy spoons into our soup. What a memorable Christmas, and not just because we celebrated in New York City when our friends graciously lent us their apartment.

Molly faced a big decision that holiday and, while maintaining her prerogative to make up her own mind, wanted to solicit our advice on the matter. Smack in the middle of her sophomore year of college, a band invited her to join them to lead worship for a Christian camp in the mountains on the weekends. The major difficulty was the seven-hour drive to and from camp. She didn't think she could manage both and do justice to either. Neither did I.

Our conversation began to take a decidedly different direction than I expected. I already knew about the band; Ron and I both saw it as a great opportunity for Molly to get to do what she's always wanted to do. And I knew it would be a stretch for her to handle school as well. But I thought she was in the process of reworking her schedule to have classes Tuesday-Thursday, that maybe she'd lighten her load for this one semester, or possibly arrange for some home study. It didn't occur to me that school would be the casualty. Nor did it seem to occur to her that she might mess up the wonderful plan I had for her life.

I'll admit to being tight-lipped and slightly ashen-faced throughout our discussion. Dear Ron, ever the optimistic encourager, asked a few questions, but I could tell he was switching sides from mine to hers faster than any swift kick I could give him under the table. Matt, in usual fashion, thoughtfully studied the issue, reluctant to land in any one camp. So I became the enemy.

Now I won't say our discussion ruined the Radio City Music Hall performance we attended later that afternoon, but I will say that the stage did not hold my attention.

Molly's decision to leave school was my first inkling that one of our kids would not carry out "the plan." So what should our attitude be when our kids go off and do something that doesn't jive with our goals for them?

We have no choice but to work with it.

First, we pray for them, dumping the whole load at God's feet because He knows just how we feel. We can get down on our knees and begin by thanking Him that He knew this all along, and He's still in control. If not in this, then in nothing.

Then, we pray for ourselves. For God's blessing on our hearts and our minds, that He will keep us from vain imaginings that only lead to stress. We pray for Him to fill up the empty rooms with smiling memories, to help us through the grocery store when we only need one of those baskets you sling through your arm instead of the huge cart. We pray that He will help us keep our eyes on Him rather than on the circumstances.

And finally, we pray for the grace to present our children and their choices to others with a smile on our face. I'll never forget the reaction *all* of my friends had to Molly's news that she was quitting school to join a band. They all thought it was wonderful, a marvelous opportunity that would help her toward maturity. Every single one of those turncoats supported her decision—and made me see things a little differently. They showed me that when a child has a few wits in her head, a recent history of decent decisions, and a terrific relationship with her family, her choices can, for the most part, be trusted.

As it turned out, that year proved to be, far and away, the very best year of her life in terms of spiritual, emotional, and physical growth. It took a complete departure from what we thought was the best *for* her, to bring out the best *in* her.

At the end of that pivotal year—for Molly *and* me — I sat down with another mother and listened to her concerns about her son who was threatening to leave college midyear just as Molly had. Every mother's bone in my body wanted to say, "Make him stay! He'll regret it the rest of his life!" But of course I couldn't say that anymore. Right in front of my eyes, my youngest child grew up, made our faith her faith, lived through loneliness and stardom as a band member, and learned how to drive in the snow.

Recharging

Modern Maturity

Others have told me time and again, "Blink and your kids will be grown." I've had such a struggle with that, wanting them around and wanting freedom from them at the same time. I'll admit to a frequent longing for the daily rhythm of mothering to be over, to wanting to sleep till my *inner* alarm went off, to desiring to be freed from making sack lunches that were nutritious as well as appetizing, to being able to take a bath without anyone wanting to join me in the bathroom. Above all, I wanted to know how Matt and Molly would turn out—to be finally free of the daily awareness that I was, in a large way, responsible for every facet of the lives of these two young people God had entrusted to us.

Then they left home. Suddenly before me lay day after day of vacation—rising at my own time, pretty much doing my own thing. The freedom was intoxicating, the opportunities unlimited, the space stimulating. The future…unsettling. I discovered I was tied not only to my children but to their lifestyles. Their early morning schedules made me get up early. The promise of their certain return every afternoon assured my productivity. Now there were no checks and balances. And the onus was on me to prove *my* maturity.

Now the question became not "How will *they* turn out," but "How will *I* turn out?" This was scary for me, the thought that I might not be disciplined enough, committed enough, or energetic enough to create a healthy existence apart from my children.

Romania

Marsha Sinetar writes, "Bland adjustment is the kiss of death to life." I know that's true. Sitting back and letting life just happen, settling into a routine not of careful choosing, but of convenience and thoughtless acquiescence, is not a healthy place to be. I know I must fight against my melancholy nature and my tendency to hole up somewhere or else I will shrivel into a little old lady way before my time.

That's the first reason I went to Romania, *my* Eastern European experience…to avoid shriveling. The second reason I went was because I didn't want my friend Vicki to go alone, and now that our kids were grown, I could get away. Vicki wanted to visit one of our church's missionaries in Bucharest, Nannette Gonzalez, and I didn't like the thought of her traveling by herself, just in case. (As if I'm some undercover superhero who could do anything constructive in an emergency. But I've always thought two heads better than one when a decision has to be made, such as which is the women's bathroom [in another language], or how do we find our connecting flight?) So I told Vicki I'd go with her. And then, another friend, Meef, decided to come along as well.

We were the Three Musketeers, but without muskets, capes, horses, or swords. We went to visit Nann and to "get our hands dirty" by participating in her ministry to the abandoned babies of Romania.

Vicki burned with a vision to reach Romania (and hence the world) for Christ, Meef's heart was broken even before we left over the plight of the babies and the orphans Nann works with, and I was just plain scared and quickly forgot why I decided to go in the first place. What on earth could *I* contribute? How would I handle the poverty and inhumane treatment I would see every day? What about the war that was raging in neighboring Yugoslavia? Most importantly, what would I do with my hair? (I know that's petty, but it did enter my mind.)

Even the idea of holding babies scared me. How would I react to them? Would I become so attached it would be painful to leave? Or worse, could they be ill enough or dirty enough that I wouldn't love them immediately and unconditionally?

All these questions assailed me and kept me awake. Basically, they addressed the very need in my life I knew I must deal with, my need to grow a thicker, slicker skin. To get out there and learn and change and risk.

∽

I read (in a book about menopause, no less) that the Chinese characters for "change" are *danger* and *opportunity*, a fitting description of what risk can mean in our lives.

All change is dangerous in some way—dangerous to the status quo, requiring a shift in belief systems or priorities, and the need to put the familiar behind. Change is rife with opportunities—to find where your strengths and weaknesses lie, to learn something new, to discover a passion for something, to see yourself rise to the occasion. Or not.

The farther away I get from childhood, from the impervious sense of adolescence and young adulthood, the safer I want to feel. It's that old control issue once more.

∽

Bucharest turned out to be a crumbling old maid, hobbled by age, inattention, and misplaced values. But though her buildings are broken down and stray dogs roam littered sidewalks, her bones are good. Her past splendor is still visible in the cobblestone streets, the beautiful old buildings, and the ancient churches that praise God by their elaborate detail, if in no other way. The biggest disappointment was the new construction, which stuck out like a professional wrestler at a tea party of aging beauties. There has apparently been no attempt to soften the contrast or blend the two eras together.

We visited in April when the tulips filled the flower beds and the lilacs spilled over the fences. Though the summers are too hot and the winters too cold, spring is lovely. The farmer's market stunned us with gorgeous flowers, huge cucumbers and radishes (Vicki said, "huge as tangerines"), amazing butter lettuce, and tomatoes that would take your breath away.

But the real breath-takers had to be the babies, most of them with the dark eyes and hair of the Gypsies, the poorer side of the Romanian population. These babies come into the hospital (ill and/or abandoned) and many never see their parents again. The hospital, understaffed and underfunded (a place where dogs roam in and out and the nurses smoke), doesn't really want anything to do with these children (who range in age from birth to toddler), so they relegate them to the far end of one of the wings. There, they get sparse attention (changed *twice a day*, seldom bathed, fed with a bottle propped up in their cribs) and rarely receive any love.

That's Nann's job, and it became ours for those two short weeks. Daily we spent several hours in the hospital bathing, changing, and playing with the babies. Each day we were witness to the myriad of changes that happen in such young lives when a starved-for-attention child becomes the center of intense focus and love. Dulled children, who rarely cried because their cries brought no one to their sides, changed into wonderfully demanding, active children who now instinctively knew that they merited attention.

One little boy I held seemed startled when I sang to him, as if he'd never heard such a thing. He looked up at me, put his tiny hand against my mouth and stared. I've never had such an audience.

A little girl came into the hospital one day with no expression on her face except sadness. She didn't cry or talk. I held her most of that day, rocking on my feet (there were no chairs), trying to elicit some sort of response. The next day, after a morning of holding and rocking, she was ready to get down in a playpen, where she played quietly, looking up often making sure I hadn't left.

We stayed in Nann's cute little apartment just down the street from Ceaucescu's palace, the second largest building in the world next to the Pentagon. Her home provided us a comfortable buffer between the good ol' USA and the squalor of Bucharest. The trip proved to be a get-your-feet-wet-in-the-real-world kind of experience and coming home at the end of the day to Nann's oasis was a blessing.

I can't honestly tell you whether or not I accomplished my initial objectives, to avoid shriveling and to grow a slicker skin. I suppose those things are more a collection of steps, an amalgamation of experiences and changes. Vicki didn't actually need me, either, but I'm glad I went. And I'm glad I don't live there like Nann does. And I'm glad I held those dear babies without fear or reluctance. And I'm so glad for…America.

Miracle Love

*E*very day in Romania I e-mailed home to Ron to tell him, firsthand and while the impression remained fresh, all I encountered in Bucharest. (He actually e-mailed back that I could bring home thirteen babies. That, and no more.) He's the first one I want to know how I'm feeling and coping, and it did seem strange to be in such a situation without him at least somewhere near. Even so, it is work for each of us to include the other in our plans and inner growth. We are two very independent people.

One of my favorite books on marriage is *The Mystery of Marriage* by Mike Mason, an exploration of the magnificence in the coming together of two people. He says that marriage isn't the combining of two worlds; it's the abandoning of the two in order that a new world might be formed. That's a big order, when you think about all the ramifications.

While I sit and stew over the need to relate in a deeper way to my husband now that our children are grown, I wonder if I actually ever wanted to go to such a level of abandonment, of dependence. Maybe abandoning *my* world would have meant he wouldn't have to abandon *his* and I'd be sucked under in a riptide of conformity to his schedule, his priorities, his way of doing things. That sometimes happens to women.

And then, of course, I allowed myself to be caught up in the put-the-children-first syndrome. It seems a natural place for a woman's priorities to fall. When the children come, and she's the only one in the house who can keep track of all the schedules, the likes and dislikes, the shampoo and the toothbrushes, it's natural to make a gradual move from "wife first" to "mom first." Actually, I think Ron counted on that. He had enough on his plate without having to worry about all the details that came naturally to me.

So off I went, peopling my world with the two little souls God gave us and settling for an occasional appearance by the one with whom I should have been most comfortable, most at home, most connected. Truly, our hearts as a couple weren't icy; we just fell into a convenient way of living. You do your thing, the kids and I will do ours. You go your way—we'll be there, somewhere, just don't expect us to throw our schedules out the window, you hear?

So now that my kids are adults, now that they're strong and healthy and happy...and gone...I'm ready to return to my first human love—and I realize with the force of a strong wind that my priorities were off center all those years.

What I did was put off the hard-work element of my marriage relationship. The struggle, when you're worn out, to make connections in the course of everyday life—in between piles of laundry, before you unload the dishwasher, during halftime, after the kids are in bed. What I didn't understand clearly was this most important point: Because God set up marriage to be the most significant human relationship between a man and a woman, a reflection of the Godhead itself, marriage is worth, and requires, every bit of energy I have to give to it.

It bothers me that I'm having this discussion with myself at this stage in our marriage—coming up on our thirtieth anniversary. These are the discussions I should have had thirty-*one* years ago, yet they involve questions I couldn't have considered then, and they suggest complications I could never have foreseen. I didn't know what I was doing. I knew nothing of the challenges of marriage, didn't know that endearing idiosyncrasies can become annoyances over time, didn't fully understand the two-shall-become-one directive. I thank God daily for linking me up with this good man who didn't give up on me. And because of that, now I'm ready to be married to him.

And now I know what else I didn't understand. That real love, healthy love, is a miracle. That when we love with abandon, when we throw every thought of ourselves out the window for the sake of the other, we get back more than we gave in the first place. When we give ourselves away in love, we are not diminished. We are expanded. We become more than it was possible for us to be alone. "To give yourself away in love to someone else," says Frederick Buechner, "is to become for the first time yourself fully."

In Sickness
and in Health

⁓

$\mathcal{I}$'ll admit that "giving myself away" rubs against some of that rugged individualism that, as an American, I have come to treasure. Independence and individualism sound like positive attributes until you look behind them at the selfishness and narcissism that appear to be the root issues.

For that reason, I've been enamored by the moving account of J. Robertson McQuilkin's resignation from the presidency of Columbia Bible College and Seminary (now Columbia International University). This academician, leader, writer, and longtime professor, stood before a college crowd and tearfully handed off his leadership of the college to another in order to go home to care for his wife, Muriel. Mother of six, a talented, busy woman with her own radio show, Muriel was diagnosed with Alzheimer's disease in her mid fifties. After some time it became clear to McQuilkin that Muriel needed him at home. She lived a happy and contented life only when he was nearby, becoming dreadfully unhappy, even frightened, without him. Listen to part of his chapel address to his faculty and students:

The decision [to leave] was made, in a way, 42 years ago when I promised to care for Muriel "in sickness and in health...till death do us part." So...as a man of my word, integrity has something to do with it. But so does fairness. She has cared for me fully and sacrificially all these years; if I cared for her for the next 40 years I would not be out of her debt. Duty, however, can be grim and stoic. But there is more: I love Muriel. She is a delight to me—her child-like dependence and confidence in me, her warm love, occasional flashes of that wit I used to relish so, her happy spirit and tough resilience in the face of her continual distressing frustration. I don't *have* to care for her. I *get* to! It is a high honor to care for so wonderful a person.

J. Robertson McQuilkin, *A Promise Kept* (Wheaton, IL: Tyndale House, 1998), pp. 22-23.

What woman doesn't want a love like that, a man ready and willing to lay down his life and his future for her? I dare say, men feel the same, if and when it should come to their minds. Such a choice doesn't often present itself in such a profoundly life-consuming way as it did with McQuilkin, with nearly half his professional life in front of him. But in many marriages, one spouse will have to set aside his or her plans in order to care for the other.

So one morning in the shower I'm thinking to myself, can I expect Ron to rise to such an occasion? Because, you see, now that our children and all the situations that came with them are not nearby anymore, our focus is shifting and the questions are changing. The future will soon be "me and thee" and, though it may feel like a betrayal to ask difficult questions that address faithfulness and steadfastness, ignoring the issues doesn't make them disappear. I recognize this may reflect my insecurities more than Ron's insensitivities. Regardless, the questions are still *in* me and in the minds of many women.

It occurs to me that I'm quite capable of just waiting for such an occasion to arise to see if, indeed, Ron *will.* And I realize that it's not fair for me to be watching and waiting, to be anticipating this life-changing test just to see if he can measure up. For that's the attitude I detect within myself. Not one of expectation, but of testing, suspicion, and challenge.

Could it be that, now that our children are nearly grown and happy and secure in life, I've been waiting to take on my husband, to make him my next project as if he needed remodeling like our bathroom? God forbid!

Sonnet 116

∽

Let me not to the marriage of true minds
Admit impediments; love is not love
Which alters when it alteration finds,
Or bends with the remover to remove.
O, no! it is an ever-fixed mark
That looks on tempests and is never shaken;
It is the star to every wand'ring bark,
Whose worth's unknown, although his height be taken.
Love's not Time's fool, though rosy lips and cheeks
Within his bending sickle's compass come;
Love alters not with his brief hours and weeks,
But bears it out even to the edge of doom.
If this be error and upon me proved,
I never writ, nor no man ever loved.

WILLIAM SHAKESPEARE

Closed-In Communion

It's been a long time in coming, but Ron and I are on a car trip together. Not a lark such as my trip with Molly—we actually thought about this one and planned some—but it is, in its own way, an adventure. We have several specific destinations—drop Molly at camp where she'll be counseling for the summer, show up at a wedding in Oregon where Matt will join us for the weekend, visit Ron's family in Washington—but everything and everywhere in between is up for grabs. We have no hotel reservations, no particular route, no kids (except here and there). And no agenda.

Except I have one. I want to work on this communication thing. Now that we'll be spending more focused time together, I want to work on building a tight relationship with this other important person in my life. It will mean the world to us and speak volumes to the neighbors. And I've decided that at some point on this trip I want to ask Ron if he will "be Robertson. McQuilken" to me. Because I want him to know what I'm thinking, and because I don't want to find myself waiting around for the "occasion to arise."

We pack. I pack the suitcase, he packs the car. I open the backdoor to slip in Molly's guitar, and there on the floor is a veritable file cabinet of materials. Up on the seat is a container of tapes and workbooks Ron wants to go through; there's his brown briefcase with his computer, his other brown briefcase with books and magazines, and his black briefcase with all the cords that feed his other electronic playmates—the cell phone, the Palm Pilot. Three briefcases. On vacation with us. I quickly pack up my computer and cords so I'll have my own ammunition.

Now, if it comes to it, we can e-mail each other.

Off we go, energized by the prospects of vacation, although with all the electronics I'm wondering just what I've gotten myself into. We drop Molly off at camp, grin at each other because we really *are* looking forward to this, and speed off up the mountain. No slim pickings from grocery store shelves for our first meal alone; we find an out-of-the way Italian restaurant, obviously popular, find a seat on the porch, and have wonderful to-die-for ravioli. We're doing this vacation thing right.

But it's the Fourth of July, and I'm itching for fireworks. We've already missed the picnics in the park and our community parade. I mention the thought to Ron, and he graciously says we'll keep our eyes open, and if we see anything, we'll stop. He's a sucker for fireworks, but absolutely detests the rigmarole that usually goes along with the show—the crowds, the waiting, the parking. I know deep down he's hoping we can just find a comfortable bed. And soon.

By 8:45 we're outside San Francisco, tired and wondering where we'll sleep, and I've given up on the fireworks. Somehow spotting them in the distance from the car window, barreling down the freeway, doesn't excite me.

So, as I'm driving, I decide it's time to look for the next "lodging" sign and take the exit. We do just that, pulling into a nondescript hotel in the middle of a block of car dealerships at 9:00. "Ask about fireworks," I say plaintively, just in case, as Ron gets out to check us in. He does (bless him) and God provides (bless Him); fireworks are six blocks away beginning in thirty minutes. We unload, change into jeans, and drive the six blocks.

We pick our way through the blankets and sleeping bags looking for a bit of grass we can call our own. I can't remember ever watching fireworks together alone; Ron stretches out, and I lie up against him with my head nestled in his waist. It's very romantic. Children (but not ours) scamper about us in the half-dark, those cool florescent tubes of chartreuse and shocking pink iridescence circling their brows. Gentle conversation ebbs and flows, blanket to blanket, friend to friend. And the show begins. We sit under the stars—both the God-made ones and the man-made ones. It's a toss-up as to which is grander. All is peaceful and beautiful until the sprinklers come on, and then, what tranquility we'd found is abruptly, rudely…washed away.

Driving back to the hotel, having found the quickest way out of the pending traffic jam, Ron comments on how great it is to avoid the hassle of previous years. We weren't even gone an hour, so unlike the big productions of the past. He loves it, I love it, we love each other. And we have a comfortable bed.

The next day, it's not long before the computer rears its little square black head. Ron is in car heaven. He's found the right connections so he can plug his computer into the cigarette lighter, and he's set to go. I'm driving, his preference and often mine. Next time I look over I see he's not struggling with the map to better figure out where we are. He's struggling to get it wedged into the passenger window to minimize the glare on his computer screen. Then another map is shoved under the visor. Now there is no glare. If I sit just right, I can see out the passenger side rearview mirror as long as he doesn't move. We ride that way for five hours. Has he ever been this productive? And does it bother me?

Not really, I'm surprised to discover. I need a little mind time, a little solitary think time, and he needs to feel connected to his busy world. And I realize this is all about compromise. This whole trip is a picture of marriage, a microcosm, a test case, an experiment of two people living closely together going the same direction.

We are very different people sharing a closed-in place. (In fiction writing, the climactic scene, the crisis, is best when it's scripted into a tight physical space to correspond with the tight emotional space.) When that's the setting, survival and civility are assured through compromise alone. Now, granted, with Ron pecking away at his computer and me thinking in my own little world, we're not having the deep, long talks I'd hoped for. Not this day. But what we're doing is *working out*. I've got him where I want him—and I know he'd pull those maps off the window and visor, unplug his computer, and focus on me if I asked him to. (Actually, I can reach the maps if I stretch a little…) And, with his work world as close as his lap, we find we can make a choice, on the spur of the moment, mind you, to extend our trip to two weeks instead of ten days. And we do.

One night at dinner, I ask Ron about Robertson McQuilken, tell him honestly what I've been thinking, and ask him openly, carefully, if he'll do that for me. He's quiet for a minute. And I know what he's thinking. He's wondering how to respond to my obvious need to know yet at the same time reserving the right to make his own decisions when the time comes. Ron does not like to be corralled into my fantasies, especially when it's possible that I've not considered all the alternatives. He asks me, "Do you think the way Robertson handled his wife's situation is the only way to go?"

But that's not what I want to hear. It's not what I'm asking. I don't want to discuss options. I want to know that he loves me enough to give up his dreams to take care of me. He's always met my needs in the past; I have no reason to doubt him in the future. In my rational mind I know he'll be there for me. In my emotional mind, however, I want to hear him *say* it.

And then I'm wondering if his question in answer to mine is indicative of too many intimate conversations delayed, or derailed, by science projects, bedtime stories, and book reports. Once again I see the results of this child-centered climate I've created that has locked him out too long.

I comfort myself with the realization that this struggle for understanding is not only a healthy step in our growing together, but also a picture of the compromise in our marriage. Not a compromise that gives up, but one that gives room and time for the other's natural responses to difficult questions.

Compromise is not another word for avoidance, or for stuffing our true feelings deep inside. At least not in our marriage. Rather it gives Ron and me the freedom to fit together into our own personal jigsaw puzzle, one that doesn't really look like any other.

It's the only way to live, daily, in a certain space with the same person. Healthy compromise is necessary because we're all good at different things, because we don't all like the same salad dressing. It makes the bathroom "share-able," the burdens bearable, and car trips a lot more fun. It gives me the freedom to ask the hard questions and gives Ron the freedom to answer them in a way that he's comfortable. And then it allows us both to talk about those questions and continue to grow into the partner the other needs.

Failing at Clay

All our lives together, Ron has encouraged me to explore my interests. He's told me time and time again that my growth is important to him. So when I get the chance I take it, if it's not too much of a risk.

September. I see not a soul on the grounds of the Colorado convent I've come to for a writer's conference. It's dark; there is a solitary bulb hanging over the backdoor of the building that is supposed to house my room…and my roommate, for that matter. We both traveled from San Diego but via different routes and on different days. She's somewhere in town but not here to greet me. No one is.

My old friend who picked me up at the airport and with whom I've spent a lovely evening is reluctant to leave me here on these rather desolate-looking grounds. But my key fits the lock, Nancy's things are proof of her arrival, and I'm brave enough to stay in this quiet, empty place.

I think.

As I'm settling in and changing into my pajamas, hanging my clothes on the rack, and putting out my toiletries, I remember all of a sudden one of the most frightening experiences of my childhood. It happened in a convent. And immediately some of those old memories assault me. It's a trick of the enemy, I know, and I don't want to give in. But I allow myself a brief revisiting of my past.

I had joined my fourth-grade Sunday school class on a sort of a field trip to a local Episcopal convent to observe the sisters in their evening vespers service. It was winter in Denver, 5:00-ish, cold, dark, and damp outside and not a whole lot different inside. The stone convent chapel, something I would consider charming and appropriate now, proved then to be rather forbidding and chilling. Of course the sisters were pleasant enough, but I was not used to the austerity of the surroundings, the chanting of the Scriptures, or the sounds of *a cappella* singing and prayer in a stone room.

We sat together as a class on wooden pews behind the sisters, a little out of place and shy, not knowing how to react and certainly not comfortable enough to join in even if we had a clue about what to do. Suddenly, with no warning whatsoever, a woman several rows behind us let out a bloodcurdling scream and fell to the floor, writhing and moaning, beating her fists on the stones. Later we learned the poor woman had had a *grand mal* epileptic seizure. Giving it a medical term did little to soften the impact.

I was completely overwhelmed with terror. Never in my life had I been witness to something that frightened me so, nor had I ever heard such a scream, nor seen a medical emergency right before my eyes. Though we continued on with the service and then a tour of the convent, I only wanted to be right next to my teacher, touching her, near enough for protection. In the dim light of the building, every shadow seemed full of menace, every doorway held untold terrors. My only memories of that convent, that vespers service, are frightening ones.

Those were the memories that assailed me that dark night. Yet as I crawled into bed with my book (one should never go anywhere without a book), with an ear open for Nancy's slight step, I resolved that this would be a different experience. And it was.

With children grown and gone, many of us former stay-at-home moms need to find things to do, places to go, old interests to awaken that we can finally develop into skills and job opportunities. We need to force ourselves into new situations and relationships, just so we don't get too comfortable. So I came here with Nancy, my role model of how to do this growing stuff.

We had joined a conference called Ad Lib, a great appellation leaving room for definition and for the unexpected. As a group of writers/artists we came together to listen and discuss and...grow. Is there any other word that says it so succinctly? And we gathered to experience the incarnational aspect of Christianity, to work out what it might mean to bring Christ into our creative expressions. I wasn't exactly sure what that meant, but I was willing to give it a try.

Partly I was willing because the older I get the more I recognize that we are wrong to completely dismiss expressions of faith from other denominations. Partly I was willing because I know instinctively that there's more to God than I now understand. Partly I was willing because I'm afraid of getting to the place where nothing is new, where I'm afraid to experiment with how I think and how I do things and what I understand about the walk of faith.

So here Nancy and I were at this new place, and I was feeling way too familiar with the convent surroundings (it wasn't the same place where I was frightened earlier, but there were some similarities), and we were meeting new people who might ask us to participate in activities that didn't belong in our comfort zones.

That's exactly what happened, of course. Initially, I was delighted! We were offered the opportunity to experiment with a different creative expression. I chose clay. And I was a failure.

Now I know—in fact, they all said it to me—that I didn't really *fail* at clay. How can you fail when your only goal is to participate and get what God wants you to get out of it? When all you're doing is experimenting? I know all that. But this is what happened. You tell me what *your* conclusions would be.

First, our instructor asked us to meditate on the theme of the conference, Psalm 62:1-2, "My soul waits in silence for God only; from Him is my salvation. He only is my rock and my salvation, my stronghold; I shall not be greatly shaken."

Then she told us to take our clump of clay and just to work it, work it, as we meditated on the scripture. Squeezing it and folding it over, pressing our thumbs deep into the center and warming it, softening it, making it pliable and workable. All the while thinking about silence, about God being our rock and salvation. And, as God led, letting the shape begin to come out of our clump of clay.

Well, frankly, at that instruction I began to get a little sweaty in the palms. Let the shape come out? God will tell me what to do? Something will arise from the lump, and it will be God's idea and I'll be His hands? "Yes," she said. "Just relax and work that clay and see how He leads you. Don't come to the clay with any preconceived ideas. Let God tell you what He wants you to sculpt."

Right, I thought. And I worked it and worked it. All around me delighted writers and dancers and painters were squishing their clay, beginning to shape recognizable images. Rapture lit up their faces and eyes, some of them even hummed softly in their own little worlds without realizing it. And it appeared as if they never stopped to think, nor did they feel the need to crumple it all up and begin again.

Me? I was working it, working it, and nothing was coming from the Lord or from my hands.

Time was up, lunch ready, and afterwards, in our free time, I took my clay to the room and worked it some more, sitting in the oversized windowsill. Once, I detected a shape that resembled the haunches of a rabbit, crouched. Maybe looking for that rock, that salvation. Then, I began to work on an image that had come to my mind long ago as I prayed one day. It was hard to sculpt, however, and when I took it outside and ran into my instructor—unfortunately—she said, "Did you think that up or did God lead you?"

Guilty, I went back to work, but I just couldn't do it. I couldn't free my mind or my spirit up, I guess. If I did sense a direction, I didn't have the talent to get there. I was failing at clay, and although I felt secure enough in myself that it wasn't terribly burdensome, I did get a little bummed by the whole thing.

The next morning in clay class I began again with a new lump. I worked it until it was supple and warm in my hands, and I meditated on our psalm. *God, You are my rock*, I prayed silently. And I made a rock with my clay.

Then I hollowed it out to make a bowl, a receptacle of the saving grace that is God's gift to me. And then, I smoothed out my rock/bowl and made my bowl…rock. Like a cradle. *God, my Rock, You rock me in Your arms like a mother does her child. Thank You.*

Then I took another lump of clay, softened it up, and right away the suggestion of a shape appeared. The cowed back of a monk, the sloped shoulders of a praying man, his mantle coming from the top of his head to the middle of his back, his arms folded in front of him, his hands clasped or maybe just hidden under his robe. The slight suggestion of eyes, nose, beard. Very primitive. Reflective of reflection, and of childlike ability. I held him up to my new friend, Ruth, whose sculpture was solid and beautiful (and recognizable), and who'd suffered in friendship at my ineptitude.

Ruth smiled with relief and said, "And so it begins." I scratched that phrase into the hem of my monk's garment. I call him ASIB. He sits on my filing cabinet and reminds me that I tried.

Frost

I experimented with travel and clay, and Molly kept on singing—through the winter, spring, and into the summer at camp with her band "How's Kelly." Then into the next fall all over the country with her new group, "Everybody-duck" (don't ask about the names).

Tacked on the bulletin board before me is a piece of cardboard, carefully cut and folded, sent to me in the fall of 1999. Inside is taped a red maple leaf and underneath are lines from Robert Frost's poem "The Road Not Taken" written in my daughter's familiar hand: "Two roads diverged in a wood, and I—I took the one less traveled by, and that has made all the difference."

Molly adds, "This leaf is from Shelbyville, Kentucky, so far the most gorgeous place I've been. Wish you were here to enjoy it with me."

Talk about two roads diverging and taking the one less traveled. Did Frost imagine the ideas he would put into the minds of the nation's young with a poem like that? Lines that would pave the way for my daughter's leaving? Lines with such whimsy and elegance and class that none of us can dismiss them?

The Road Not Taken

Two roads diverged in a yellow wood,
And sorry I could not travel both
And be one traveler, long I stood
And looked down one as far as I could
To where it bent in the undergrowth;

Then took the other, as just as fair,
And having perhaps the better claim,
Because it was grassy and wanted wear;
Though as for that the passing there
Had worn them really about the same,

And both that morning equally lay
In leaves no step had trodden black.
Oh, I kept the first for another day!
Yet knowing how way leads on to way,
I doubted if I should ever come back.

I shall be telling this with a sigh
Somewhere ages and ages hence:
Two roads diverged in a wood, and I—
I took the one less traveled by,
And that has made all the difference.

ROBERT FROST

Home Again, Home Again, Jiggity Jig

While I began my emancipation from the home front and Molly toured the country, making a living and living her dream, Matt got stuck…at home.

After college he *chose* to come home for a year to work with Ron, doing some grunt work, to be sure, but also learning much about management and computers. However, as the months dragged on he began to struggle with his future plans, with the closeness of living at home with his parents, with not being able to see or discern any specific vision for his life. He seemed happy enough here—we did our best to stay removed from at least some of his life—but he knew it would be healthier for him to move out and be on his own. We agreed.

Time and time again, trying always to choose the right moment, when Matt's heart and stomach were full, I brought up the subject of his moving out. Several of his friends were living at home—"get them together and find a place," I said, as if it had never occurred to him. "Go back east and visit your old friend Cameron. Move in with him for a while. Move to Boulder with Ben for a season. I love you and have a wonderful plan for your life."

(The week before Christmas I shared a holiday lunch with five other women friends. What fun. We all have sons near the same age and have known one another for some years. As we chatted around the table, we found that every one of us had at least one son, graduated from college, living at home. Boomerang kids.)

Why are we so itchy to get our kids out and on their own? Most parents I know wince at the thought of boomerang kids. It's become one of those roll-your-eyes-over-your-coffee conversations. It's the new major prayer concern of baby-boomer moms. It's even a hot Internet topic.

But I want to know where this urge to purge comes from. The more I think about it, the more I suspect it's another of those late-twentieth-century expectations. The American Dream. Buy a house and an SUV, have two-and-a-third children, find a dog at the pound. Raise your kids to be professionals and Internet savvy, send them off to college, and get them grounded in the world. (And the Word. After all, this is a Christian dream as well.) Once they're gone, they'll still *need* you, of course, but don't take them back home…or they'll never leave.

When did we stop planning for the "& Son" to be added to the sign above the family store? Why aren't the children standing in line to take over the farms, the dental offices, the construction jobs? What made us Americans so enamored with the idea of independence that we encourage our kids to take off as soon as they reach a certain age?

I suspect the idea began with the industrial revolution and reached maturity with the urbanization of our country, when the fathers began reporting somewhere other than their home fields for work. Once the dads were off the premises, the sons didn't need to stay around either. Or the daughters.

But I think this is a very Western idea.

In many cultures around the world today, sons bring their new brides back home to the family residence. On a recent trip to Jerusalem with our church, Ron and I saw houses with steel rods extending straight up from the roof in preparation for another floor, the newlywed's first home. I guess "leave and cleave" is more a question of mind-set and attitude than geography.

These were all new thoughts for me, and they came just in time to ready me to hear what Matt had been thinking. On New Year's Day we were in the car alone. It was gray and drizzly out—I loved it—and I brought up *again* the "go here, do that" comments for which I'm so famous. But today we took time to hear each other.

"Some of my friends would suggest we give you a date to be out," I said.

"Don't do it," he said. "It's not what I need."

Then he explained what he had been wrestling with. And it all came down to this: He sensed that *God* had told him to wait, to stay where he was, to specifically *not* move out of our house.

And then I realized that what we were talking about was obedience. Matt didn't want to be living at home; he didn't want to seem indecisive about his future; he was more than ready to get going. But he was choosing to be obedient to the leading of God in his life and, frankly, Ron and I had no right to interfere. It was illuminating. Finally the onus was off us as parents and off Matt as a young adult. We were waiting for God. And I felt a freedom to let Matt stay on at home, in his room, for as long as it took. Ron agreed.

Interestingly, the next day I stumbled upon an Internet article that separated boomerang kids into "planners" and "strugglers." The planners use the home front strategically, to save money, to have a cushion of safety and counsel while they prepare for the world. The strugglers come home out of necessity because they're not sure of themselves yet. Often they have no plans for the future, other than living at home for a while.

I will add a third category, that of "waiters," and I don't mean the kind with trays in their hands. These are the kids, like Matt, who are waiting for God's direction, who want to move ahead yet don't have the freedom or the leading to make the move.

I don't know really what to do about it, except become a waiter, too. It's a good place to be, waiting on the Lord. He tells us to do it, promises that those who wait on Him "will gain new strength; they will mount up with wings like eagles, they will run and not get tired, they will walk and not become weary" (Isaiah 40:31). I'll wait. I *like* those words.

My Knight of Knights

Molly got a break from the road and came home for the holidays, so we are all here together. That's my greatest present this year. And then comes the night of our thirtieth anniversary, December 27, 1999. For years our anniversary has been lost in the wrappings and trappings of Christmas. Now and then we'd go out for a quick dinner; once we went to a musical review. But mostly we let the day pass and stayed home to relax and unwind with the kids. Ron was occasionally out of town.

This year I'm determined to make the most of the moment. Somehow thirty years has such a punch to it, and to celebrate just four days before the year 2000 gives this anniversary extra importance. So I call friends, and Ron scours the Internet, for a cool place to celebrate. We invite two other couples and Matt and Molly and make reservations for an over-priced landmark restaurant in downtown San Diego. I'd wanted to *have* to dress up, but a place that requires dressing up is hard to find in this city by the sea, where shorts are accepted nearly everywhere all year, and all night, long. I find that the only dress-up restaurants around cost at least $50 per person. That seems a little extravagant, even for the thirtieth. As it is, we dress down, pay less, and, as is nearly always the case, the company makes the meal. We love being together with our friends; particularly we love it that our kids are also our friends and seem to belong in this gathering of adults.

In the past, Ron and I've pretty much overlooked anniversary gifts, unless something just happened to catch our fancy at the last minute. Except for one year—our twentieth anniversary. On December 7, 1989, Ron presented me with the first of twenty small gifts, one for every year of marriage. It blew me away. They ranged from little china figurines all the way to a full-sized easel as I was doing some oil painting at that time of my life.

So this year—not that long after I challenged Ron to "be Robertson McQuilkin" for me—it seemed important that I not let the day pass by without something special from me to him. Something symbolic that confirms to him that I trust his faithfulness and love. I found it just before Christmas in the mall—an eight-inch-tall knight with a shield bearing a cross on it. He has a scowl on his face, which Ron rarely does, but aside from that he's just right, a perfect representation of what I appreciate the most in my husband. Protection, a covering, steadiness, a point man standing in the gap for his wife and family. Willing to fight large dragons and forage for food, and to walk the castle walls with an eye out for the enemy.

It's so easy for us women to wish our husbands would change—be some kind of a fantasy guy who looks and acts like Harrison Ford. We overlook the fact that leadership, that godly "husbanding," is a quality based on character and not on personality or even ability. After all our discussion about Robertson McQuilken's sacrificial love for Muriel, I realized that Ron needed to hear me say that

I approve of him, that I know he is a good man (in fact the best man I know), and that I know he will be my knight when I need him to be.

Now, more than ever, I needed to say it and he needed to hear it, because, once again, our kids are not around often enough to validate him or to distract me. I cannot bury myself in their lives if I'm feeling neglected or unloved; he cannot live on their affection alone if he's feeling unappreciated. All we have is each other. And it's important that we are enough.

The Grace That Goes Before

January 2000. It's winter here, according to the calendar. Winter in spring's clothing. Although overcast skies gray the day, it's warm and humid. No seasons for us in Southern California. I find it way too boring. Will we ever have rain?

I catch a movement out the sliding glass doors. Oh, wow! The hummingbird mom is back. I didn't expect her until February; she's two weeks early. And I really didn't expect to catch her at her important business of nest building.

I look up into the creeping fig that blankets our trellis and provides a nearly impenetrable roof for our patio, and find the crooked branch that she's targeted. Already there are bits of a chalky substance clinging there. It hardly seems possible…yet by the afternoon I see a cup-shaped home, not big enough yet, not tall enough, nor protective enough, but definitely there. It's a miracle.

Today I watch her swoop in with a bit of fluff in her beak. She tucks it in place, doing whatever she does to cement it hard. In three days the tiny cup is large enough to cradle this tiny, pregnant bird.

This little mother has gone before her family, has prepared a place for them to be born and grow and leave. Sounds all too familiar.

The same few days I'm watching this mother hummingbird preparing her nest to lay, raise, and shoo away her babies, I'm also having soul-searching conversations with my children about their futures.

Both Matt and Molly are at the leaving stage, at crossroads in their lives. And these aren't "where to go to college" conversations we're having; they're way beyond that one. Both have big decisions to make, the kinds of determinations that could decide the course of their lives. Of course, in Robert Frost's inimitable words, " knowing how way leads on to way," what they choose now *will* affect the rest of their lives. More than ever their futures are indecipherable to Ron and me. And probably to them.

Molly has just informed us of her desire to find an apartment in another city and to go back to school to be closer to her boyfriend. Her *boyfriend*?

And Matt. For nearly six months he has been waiting patiently, and now and then not so patiently, for God to make it clear where he is to go. Now he tells me he's moving to the Philippines, thousands of miles across the globe. "Too much money away," as a friend of mine once said.

Yesterday he made his final commitment to this move. Ron is thrilled as Matt will still be working with him, albeit by telecommunications. I think it's a positive move, too, but all evening my eyes filled up with self-pity tears as I dwelt on the sweet months we've had together day after day and the looming distance that will separate us soon. And I finished Frost's poem in my mind, over and over—"I doubted if I should ever come back." How maudlin is that?

Very, very soon (and I've said this before) they will be gone. To places I can't prepare ahead of time.

Recently, I've been introduced to the concept of "prevenient" grace, "the grace that goes before." Deuteronomy 31:8 in a word: "The LORD is the one who goes ahead of you; He will be with you. He will not fail or forsake you. Do not fear, or be dismayed."

Perfect timing, this new theological term. I love it how God brings these things up just when we need them. Is that prevenient grace, too? I think so.

This is what I cling to: the promise that God goes ahead and prepares the way for us. If this is true, it means God is working out the details for Matt in the Philippines already. And, because He has a mother's heart, it means He's doing it in a way that will meet even what *I* think Matt needs. Now that's comforting.

Molly's not going so far away, just a few hundred miles. However, she's going towards a young man. A good man, but someone I don't know *quite* well enough yet. Does God's prevenient grace apply here, in matters of the heart? It better. And if I am to let her go, if I am to trust God in her life, I must let her make this move with all the encouragement I can manage.

I'm glad to know that God's prevenient grace will go before *me,* too. It will be there when I'm lonely and can't quite remember where their freckles are. It will be there when I wish they were around to provide an excuse to stay home. It will be there in full force when Ron's gone, the house is quiet, and I let my melancholy genes take over. I'm not sure yet exactly what my life will be like. But certainly if I can trust God in my kids' lives, I can trust Him in mine.

Reaffirming

Jesse

✑

hough I thought car trips with Molly were history, every now and then an occasion arises that puts us together again in a tight, closed environment, moving at a rapid pace. This time it was a brand-new experience because our driving took us to the young man who'd stolen Molly's heart.

"He's twenty-six," she told me hesitantly when we talked that summer of their meeting, and she only twenty.

"Twenty-six!" I shouted over the phone.

"That's okay, Mom. He doesn't act it."

Was that supposed to be reassuring?

And now, after months of watching this friendship bud and blossom into romance, we were en route to his hometown for a visit. Talk about teachable moments. This went way beyond that. A whole teachable twenty-four hours. She peppered me with questions about my marriage, about marriage in general. We talked about the kinds of men that strike fear in a mother's heart—men who want to be mothered rather than married, men who can't control their anger, men who don't care to learn how to communicate with their wives, men who keep their wives in poverty. We talked about what it means to be a wife, how to go about supporting and respecting a husband without losing your own identity. We talked about time, and how important it would be to take all the time needed for both of them to be sure of each other. And we talked about how this one decision, second only to a decision to follow Jesus, is the absolute most important one a man and woman can ever make.

I did all the driving, and I could feel Molly's eyes on me, intent on what I had to say, eager to pick up any nuance that might escape through a facial expression or shift of the eyes. Every now and then we'd look at each other and giggle, that nervous laugh that said, I can't believe we're talking about this!

We met Jesse for dinner, and our time together confirmed all I'd heard about him…that he's kind, smart, talented, committed, funny, growing in godliness, not given to anger. He's not like Ron in personality—much more like me. That gave me pause. I have been so built up and gently polished by Ron's sunny persona, I wish it for everyone.

And then I realized I wanted Molly to marry…Ron. I wanted her to marry a man just like mine.

When I finally admitted it, peace settled over me like sunshine when the clouds move on. Molly doesn't need Ron, she needs Jesse. And vice versa. I can see it. I can tell that they will be better, more productive, more effective— happier—together than apart. What more could *any of us* want for our children?

Smiling Easter Eyes

*E*aster 2000, one week before Matt leaves. Tulips are scattered in vases around the house. Outside it's cool and misty but promises to be warm and sunny by the time church is over. We're having a leisurely family breakfast around the dining room table. God has graciously revived the bushy bougainvillea that my dear husband, prone to pruning, cut back to near extinction four years ago. Several of its blooming branches spread from a rose bowl along the center of the dining room table in quiet yet glorious testimony to resurrection.

But more beautiful yet are the smiling eyes around the table. Ron at the other end across from me; Molly and Jesse on one side of us, Matt and his new girlfriend on the other. Ron asks me to bless our breakfast, and I stumble all over myself with verbal and heartfelt gratitude for the two couples at our table, more specifically for the two *new* people who've brought such happiness to our own children and, thereby, to us.

At church we take up the entire length of one of the shorter pews, and I can't wipe the smile off my face as I glance down the row and see all the fingers interlaced. Indeed, my heart is overflowing this resurrection Sunday, knowing full well that the abundance we're experiencing in our family is due to the loving grace of Jesus, who died for us all and taught us by His example and words what is of supreme value in this life.

But that's not all that happens this weekend. The next morning, right after my kickboxing class, I meet with Ron and Jesse at our local breakfast place. This is *the* talk, the one where Jesse asks us for permission to marry our daughter. We know what's on his mind, and he knows we know, and we know he knows we know. Still he's a little nervous and I am...well, not nervous but antsy. I want to ask the right questions and respond in a way that will encourage him...but not let him entirely off the hook.

Thanks to Ron—and to Jesse's openness—I think we do it right. Ron peppers him with questions about strengths and weaknesses, hopes and goals, future plans and finances. Finally, just as we're getting up to leave, Jesse says, "I suppose I should actually ask the question. May I have your daughter's hand in marriage?"

Ron looks at me. "What do you think, Mar? Shall we give him the thumbs up or down?"

Poor Jesse. Does he know what he's getting into?

Roosters and Basketball

Matt flew off one month ago today. Though there have been occasions when I've nearly called out his name to read him something interesting, now I just sit at my computer and type it all out to send with the next e-mail. God bless electronics.

We've even spoken several times, when it's late afternoon here and the next morning there. Last time we talked the roosters in his neighborhood were making such a racket they were bothering *me*, thousands of miles away! Turns out, as he discovered later, these are prized fighting cocks.

God's prevenient grace is all over Matt's life, and I'm embarrassed to say I can't get over it. I should have expected our extravagant God to act in an extravagant way in response to my specific prayers for his housing, his relationships, his transition. Because here is what God did, in both my words and Matt's: He set Matt up in a roomy duplex; his space adjoins that of another missionary couple who he really likes. He gave Matt a "nice, big, fat lawn and a half-court for basketball" and two college-age boys down the street to play ball with, sons of one of the Christian leaders with whom he works. "They have been one of the greatest graces, because after interacting with thirty-to fifty-year-olds all day, it really helps to have some young blood." Though God has chosen to ask him to live alone, he is "already developing rich relationships" with his extended team, and there is enough activity in and out of his home that he's "not majorly lonely"; he is only a short walk from his office and, get this, has the traditional Philippine part-time helper to do laundry, grocery shopping, and cooking. Best of all, God gave Matt a place to walk and pray and keep his spiritual life healthy.

Perhaps I'm so amazed at these answers to prayer because I'm so completely out of the loop. I don't know if anything has changed as much in my relationship with my children as the way I pray. I've prayed for transitions and relationships and even housing before, but I've always had some element of control, or at least visual confirmation. I've been able to see the housing choices, participate in the purchase of sheets and towels, give approval to the neighborhoods or the roommates. Or not. But there comes a time in our children's lives when either they won't permit such scrutiny or distance prevents it.

I keep thinking all along that the interesting twists and turns in Matt's and Molly's lives are even more directly aimed at me. What God did for Matt was so far beyond "whatever I could ask or imagine" that it has encouraged both of us to believe Him for more. I think *that's* what He had in mind.

The Night Watches

When you think of it, when you put it all together—our age and stage in life, the escapades and choices of our children, the need we all have to continue to grow—handing off our children to God is a prime opportunity for us as parents. Anytime we have to trust God with those we love and have little or no occasion (or invitation) to get involved in their lives, it gives us the chance to become more than we are. And God gives us the choice of either embracing those times or turning away from them.

I'm finding within myself a greater longing than I've ever had before to know God as the provider and protector of my children. I'm really letting go now, handing off, releasing the tension that comes with watching over a child. God has wanted that releasing from me for a long time, and I've been too reluctant, or too afraid, to let Him take over. But I'm tired of all that work, all those sleepless nights, the knot in my stomach. And I'm learning what it means to meditate on the Lord.

Just the other day, as I found my stomach churning over the concerns of one of my children, I read Psalm 63:6, "When I remember Thee on my bed, I meditate on

Thee in the night watches." I'm sure I've read this psalm a thousand times. But what struck me at this reading was that, when I'm awake and troubled "in the night watches," I don't "meditate on Thee." I fret and worry first. Then I pray...if I'm feeling particularly spiritual. Prayer, of course, is well and good. But there are times when praying increases my anxiety rather than calms me, times when prayer puts the focus on the problem rather than the God of solutions.

When I make the choice to concentrate on the characterstics of God—not what He's done or what I want Him to do but on His very nature—I can't help but release a great deal of the tension I'm living under. And when there is no opportunity to cradle a troubled face, take a car trip, or shave a head, no physical or eye contact, what else can I do?

"That's the point," God is saying to me. "I'm enough. I can do it. My plans are set and better than yours. So let go."

❧

Then, the next morning, I'm on the phone with Molly, who's in a bit of a crisis. She is crying, frustrated, unsure of the future. This day I have something special, something God-given, to tell her. Meditate on the character of God, I say. Stop focusing on the problem, even in prayer, and think about who God is—His grace and goodness, His kindness and mercy, His sovereignty and power. His ability to work things out.

A day later when we talk again, I can hear the lightness in her heart over the phone.

Living Alone Together

ꚺ

Sometimes I write in light of the growth I've seen in myself; sometimes I write in anticipation of it. And other times, this being one of them, I write with a hope, but also a wistful shaking of my head.

The topic is living alone together, becoming a couple once again, childless in one very significant sense. From here on out, our children will drop in only occasionally, and Ron and I will have to learn to grow and change without them present as goads, sounding boards, accountability partners, or witnesses.

Parenting becomes a habit in the sense that we come to the place where the daily routine is just that...daily and routine. Parenting fills our time and our minds and determines our vacations, goals, and mealtimes. But one day, things change.

Now just two of us rule the roost. We can decide at a moment's notice to stick the lettuce and chicken breasts back in the fridge and take off for fish tacos, or we can sleep an entire weekend away should it suit our fancy. No one is checking up on us to see if we're eating ice cream out of the container in the middle of the night...or making love in the middle of the day, for that matter.

Not that any of the above are unsuitable for old married couples like us, but...I have a hankering for something more.

Not long ago I met a couple on our trip to Israel, Steve and Marianne. They are childless, in their forties, married sixteen years. And they know everything. They had taken time to study for our trip, familiarizing themselves with all the places we'd go. Their questions were relevant and added to the discussion. I, on the other hand, kept asking, "Now, *where* are we?"

Steve and Marianne know a lot about flora and fauna and could identify most of the flowers and trees we saw. They understood the historical significance of every ruin, and I wouldn't be surprised if they picked up some Hebrew while they were there. What I loved about them was their eagerness, both of them, to participate in every aspect of the experience. Together they *learn*. I want us to be like that when we grow up.

This is, in my mind, our biggest challenge as newly freed parents. Finding some common ground of interest that has nothing to do with work. Something that will be interesting and compelling enough to hold us and engage us to the point of mastery. Together.

But here's my dilemma in a "nutshell" story: This morning, as my coffee was warming up in the microwave, I went in as I always do to greet Ron, who'd been up long before me. Seated at his computer, of course, he delightedly explained that he'd figured out how to play movies from his new digital movie camera on his screen. Then he told me he'd configured his screen so he can work while at the same time project CNN in the upper left-hand corner. Now he has movies, TV, and work in one convenient location.

"Ah," I said. "And you don't even need a remote."

"Oh, but I *have* one," he said. And he held up *another* remote control device.

What on earth can I find that will entice Ron enough to pull him away from his computer?

✒

In thumbing through Ed Wheat's *Love Life for Every Married Couple*, I discover that what I'm longing for is an increased sense of *phileo* love in our marriage, that cherishing love characterized by friendship and sharing. Wheat says,

> But *phileo* is by no means a sure thing. It cannot be counted on as a built-in benefit of marriage….I have observed that *phileo* seems strangely absent from many marriages. Through neglect couples have lost the rapport they once had.
>
> Ed Wheat, *Love Life for Every Married Couple* (Grand Rapids, MI: Zondervan, 1980), p. 106.

We just may be guilty of the "loss of rapport." I don't think we were ever aware of it happening; it's just that as the kids were born and grew and we added soccer balls and tutus to our household belongings, *we* became less of a unit. I'd feel terrible about it if I thought we were alone in this, if all other connections we began with had deteriorated, or if there were no hope for a change. But as I read Wheat's book this afternoon, as I took some time to think about our lives and the timing of things and what outside interests we just might agree to explore, I detected a little glimmer of eagerness in myself, a tiny hopeful shoot of green growth.

I think we can do this. If I can just get rid of that remote.

New Life

⁓

Memorial Day 2000. What a glorious morning to wake up. A morning of sweet mourning, remembering the sacrifices of those who died to keep us free. So much of what we enjoy in our country would not be ours without their service. I don't suppose I can give veterans credit for the perfect weather, but somehow I feel they deserve it.

The neighborhood is quiet as I walk my customary route. The dogs are even respectful, and the huge, raucous crows that seem to multiply daily are off...multiplying, I guess. Only the sweet songbirds break the silence. What a relief.

For the first Memorial Day in a long time, we are not scheduled to be somewhere or host a party. I feel a little guilty about that. But not for long. Recently I've spent a hundred dollars on flats of flowers for our back yard and today—yes, today—Ron and I are going to plant them in a show of solidarity and oneness. I suppose yard work is more a Labor Day, or Arbor Day, activity. But not for us, not this time.

Ron begins by bringing out the long pruning saw, perfect for felling the fruit off our palm tree that otherwise would fall unbidden and crush the soon-to-be-planted new flowers. Ron prunes under my watchful eye these days, because he has a reputation for hacking away with great abandon. (There was that time he was up a ladder trimming a young silver dollar eucalyptus tree on the crest of our backyard bank. I looked away, and when I turned back, he, the ladder, *and the tree* had disappeared down the slope. Once I found out he was unhurt, I couldn't stop laughing. Neither could he.)

This time he does a masterful job, and we are both glad to have that heavy fruit down from above our heads. Then he upends the bags of topsoil we need to perk up the beds, and I get down to the planting. Petunias, alyssum, dwarf phlox, vinca, and a tall thing with starlike blooms. I have no master plan for all we're putting in: I only know that the colors are wonderful and that I want instant gratification—beds loaded with flowers as if they'd been tended regularly by pros.

We both get dirt on our knees and under our fingernails, get sunburn on our necks and the crowns of our heads. We talk a little, but not too much. We grunt with every stoop and rising, and at the end of the day our backs ache. It takes us one more afternoon to use up all the flowers I've bought, to transplant an agapanthus or two, chop down an unwanted palm, and clean up all the little containers and white plastic tags (which I should have kept somewhere so I know what those tall things with the starlike blooms are). The wonderland we create pleases us to no end, particularly because we did it ourselves.

But what I like the best is that we did it together. And now, with a parent's passion, we walk out there every day and pinch the blooms on the petunias, check the sprinklers, trim the geraniums.

This is what I want for the two of us. New life, growth, creativity, nurture, togetherness.

The Perfect Morn

 ∽

So after all these years of living in light of our children's timetable and living in fear of *not* having to live that way—imagining myself sleeping till noon and wasting the entire last half of my life—I find myself with the perfect schedule. It's mine thanks to all those years of having to get up early to get everyone out the door, fed, clean, and happy. Everyday I thank God that He has me at this place in my life.

I would have told you years before that I'm a night person. Then I became a midday person. I wanted to go to bed early and sleep in every day. I was a picture of the exhaustion of motherhood. Now I am a morning person—by choice—and it continues to amaze me. But I love it!

I don't know yet how I will turn out or whether I will grow into a crotchety old lady someday (because I can succumb to some of those tendencies even now). But I'm finally at peace knowing that I *like* getting up early and will not spend the day with bonbons and soap operas. I never want to return to the adolescent's sleep-till-noon pattern again. I can't tell you how relieved I am.

Now, the early morning is a gift to me. Whether it's dark or dawn, foggy or clear, I cherish that time. My chair faces the east, and often I see the sun begin to color the sky. I wrap up in a blanket with a hot cup of coffee on the nearby table. I read and pray and think and try to sit silently before God, wanting so much to know if He has anything special to say to me. He has blessed me with a flexible enough schedule that I get to sit that way for an hour or two, virtually uninterrupted. Then I take a walk for another hour, thinking, praying through prayer cards to keep me from being distracted (as I am so easily).

It wasn't always this way. I've struggled most of my adult life with fitting in my quiet times, and I've never had a consistent exercise program. My kids eased me into this time schedule, and now in their absence, God is turning it into the most significant time of every day.

Other than the present health and happiness of my marriage and our children, this is God's greatest gift to me. One of our many houseguests called me disciplined when she watched me walk out the door morning after morning following my quiet time. Is this discipline when it's what you long for, when you don't *want* to skip a day?

∽

One morning, wanting to hear God's voice on a particular issue, I sat quietly in my chair and put forth my question: Should we expand and remodel our bathroom, adding that bathtub I've been wanting?

I was reading in Isaiah at the time and turned to chapter 5. This is what the Lord said to me and what I took from verse 8: "Woe to those who add house to house and join field to field, until there is no more room..." Woe to me if I add to our bathroom? Then in verse 10: "For ten acres of vineyard will yield only one bath of wine…" Only one *bath*?

Granted, this sounds ludicrous here, out of the context of quiet and prayer and faith. But, I tell you, I heard God saying, "*Not yet. Not now. Wait.*" Could be, He even said *no*.

Then the next morning Molly called. "Jesse and I want to get married in December," she said. And I knew God had been speaking to me. No way could we afford a wedding and a remodeled bathroom in the same year.

The Final Separation

~

$\mathcal{A}$lthough it sometimes feels as though I've been hit by a brick with this "letting go" thing, and loneliness, even purposelessness, assail me, so far each time the separations occur there also seem to be returns, reconnections.

This time the coming-back heralded amazing plans. Molly's wedding. *Her wedding*. December date set; eight months away. So much to do and so little time.

We walk into a bridal salon, selected from a magazine. We really don't know what to expect. I've been married thirty years. I can't remember. I'm just thinking "expensive." The salon is small; we're immediately greeted by an older woman who looks like she knows what she's doing. Good. We show her a picture of a dress Molly loves. "I have that dress right here," she says, and sure enough, in moments it's hanging before us. We're encouraged. Pawing through the rack of plastic-encased gowns—beads and pearls, satin and silk, tulle and ribbons, bows and bustles—we pull out a total of eight styles, white and cream, full skirted and A-line. Then, into the long, narrow dressing room. Molly dons a long-line bra, regrets aloud wearing rather ratty navy blue underwear, and slips the first gown over her head, the one in the magazine. "That's the one I want," she had said to me when I showed her the picture. And here it is, on her slender, girlish, womanly body. This is my little girl. This is Jesse's wife-to-be.

We walk out to the platform where all the brides must stand. Mirrors are everywhere. Molly steps up onto the round riser so her dress will fall unhindered past her feet. The woman helping us clips it in the back so it fits her. She looks marvelous. Her small waist is nipped, the heavy silk skirt lies in wide, voluptuous box pleats from the fitted bodice, spaghetti straps run over her sunburned shoulders not quite fitting into the white lines left by her bathing suit.

We are both nearly speechless by how beautiful she looks, what a princess she is—she who prefers thrift store T-shirts to designer dresses. Except not this time.

Back in the dressing room, because it would be silly to buy the first thing we see, she slips on a candlelight silk—another plain, fitted bodice with just a smidge of beading around the edge, dropped waist stitched down into a point, and a skirt so voluminous it would dress a king-size bed. We are stunned. It is too beautiful to look at. Surely, not everything she puts on will tempt us so.

And of course they don't. And we don't buy the first one we see, or want, and we drive, and she puts countless dresses on over her head, pulls up full slips and fastens all sorts of bras, looks beautiful in nearly everything she tries. We talk to bridal consultants—one says she should wear ivory, another white. One says gloves, another not. We learn the terms, determine to be kind and patient with all who help us. Discretely we check out price tags and pretend that a dress for thousands of dollars is within our budget. By the end of the day, we're a little discouraged. It seems the simpler the gown, the more it costs. We don't understand.

For the next few days we drop in at all sorts of bridal salons, the ones with racks and racks in all sizes, the smaller ones with designer gowns all in size ten. We briefly consider getting it made; we look at our schedules to carve out time for the drive to the fabric houses in Los Angeles.

Then, *then*, one afternoon we slip into a small shop on the spur of the moment, just because it's *there* next to the big one where we were disappointed again. "I think I have what you want," the saleswoman says. Out comes a knock-off of Molly's dream dress at one-third the price. No one but an expert could tell the difference. We're speechless, grateful, and relieved. God is good, even down to the details.

A wedding dress is just the right costume for the ultimate send-off, the final separation. Our daughters should be wearing beautiful gowns that emphasize their departure from girlhood and their entrance into marriage.

Marriage is the ultimate closure, the permanent nest robber, or at least it should be. We ought to be able to give our children away to their spouses, expecting them to stay put, be happy, procreate.

This time in our lives as parents is the ultimate test of whether we have really cut those apron strings. They are cleaving; we parents are the ones who are left.

But it's such a good thing, when all the particulars are positive and fitting into place. As bittersweet as it will be to see Molly walking down the aisle on Ron's arm, she's walking to a young man I love as my own. A man I trust. I can't wait...I think.

Urgent Care

I really thought this part of mothering was over! This worry, this waking up in the middle of the night. This agonizing over whether to go to the doctor or wait it out. This constant temperature-taking, fluid-pouring, hand-holding part of being a mom.

But it's not over yet. Molly came home over the weekend, for thirty-six hours, to be a bridesmaid. She rolled in at 4:30 A.M. Saturday morning, cheerfully woke me with a big hug so I'd know she'd made it safely, let me *feel* her engagement ring (which I hadn't yet seen) so we didn't have to turn on the light, and plopped into bed for a few hours.

Then, after a day of bridesmaid stuff, she limped into the house, in tears, feverish and unhappy. Back to the old relationship we went, a "cryable" child, a worried mom. The swollen glands in her neck looked like buried pearls, and I flew to conclusions.

Remember, hovering's my gift.

In light of Molly's schedule—the wedding she had to sing for, her commitment to her band in the mountains, and her midnight drive returning to camp—I took her to urgent care one more time Sunday morning. Déjà vu. She had a virus, but not mono as she feared, and the doctor pronounced her "severely dehydrated." He kept her there, on a gurney, until she'd had two bags of fluids deposited intravenously into her weak little body.

But here's the cool thing: As I sat beside her bed watching the color return to her face she said, "I don't want to hurt your feelings, but I couldn't decide whether I wanted to be with you more or with Jesse." I know I smiled, because I'm actually ready for someone to take over these weekend trips to urgent care.

I Didn't

to Elizabeth

If you think I did
You're wrong
I didn't do it
I didn't do it at all

I left the glass just where you
put it down
I didn't wash it
I didn't put it away in its place
on the papered shelf
I left the lipstick kiss on the rim
And didn't even try to wipe it clean
Linens are still in disarray
on the bed
Piled with pillows like folded stones
round and heaped up
Small monuments to your presence
yesterday
I didn't wash them
I didn't hang them outside on the line
I didn't move them at all

Your book a little pyramid
on the coffee table
Where your hands abandoned it
Inside out and upside down
Like my home
Like my heart
My daughter
When you leave

—Judith Gillis

143

Teachable Moments

"Teachable moments" is one of those catch phrases that haunted us as we raised our kids. Don't miss them! Pay attention! Drop what you're doing and teach!

We all learn more effectively when our interest is piqued or we're at a needy point. I just learned how to make chili rellenos last week, for heaven's sake. Because I really wanted to know.

I thought teachable moments would taper off to nonexistent by the time I had grown children. But I'm finding it's far different. All of a sudden, our kids are coming after information and help.

Case in point, Molly's relationship with Jesse and her soon-to-be-married life. Almost daily we talk about the two of them—about what it means to be the chief supporter for a man, about working hard to remain pure before the wedding, about cooking and cleaning. It's astonishing to me how much more quickly I'm getting through to her and how eager she is to learn.

And Matt, who's off in the Philippines, is more independent than he's ever had to be. Often he shares his heart with me in e-mails and provokes a response on the line of a teachable moment. He's so receptive, so willing to hear what I have to say. Since he's reached adulthood, he's been like that, but even more so now that we do it through e-mail and he's too far away to catch my body language and tone of voice.

It encourages me so much because I have regrets. All parents do. I don't regret that our kids were able to go on missions trips during the summer, but I'm concerned that because we encouraged such involvement they never had those early, good, solid work experiences that prepare one for the real world. I don't regret that we ate out a little too often, but that I didn't place enough value on learning to cook well. I'm glad I made them do their own laundry from junior high school on, but I wish I'd made them do more housework. The piano lessons they had as children have enriched their lives; I wish I hadn't let them quit so soon!

But the very cool thing is that they recognize their limitations and, although I suppose they grumble about their ill-preparedness to their friends, they're not too hard on us as parents for getting them into this predicament. Because what we *did* do right was let them know always how loved and valuable they were and are to us. More than my next breath, I used to say to them. *That* they learned.

Rekindling

Scooters and Haircuts

Ron has this dinky little motor scooter, a Honda-150. To a guy, a Honda-150 is a step or two up from a moped, barely a "bike" at all. To a woman, it's a full-fledged motorcycle that requires a helmet and a few phrases like "be careful." Ron drives it around our neighborhood, rarely going more than 45 mph or five miles in any direction, and seldom takes it on the freeway.

He uses this bike to entertain our nieces and nephews when they come to visit and, I suppose, to entertain himself. He has a difficult time enticing me to ride with him. Really, it's not because of the danger. It's because of the helmets. What a job they do on my hair.

But now in the freedom of my fifties, now that our children are safely grown and committed to other adults who can share the responsibility of their care—and now with the freedom of my new short haircut—I'm riding with him. I'm his moll.

The other day after church we scurried home to change into shorts and rode the Honda into town for a street fair. The scooter makes for wonderful convenience. Parking is never a problem. I pulled off my black helmet, fluffed my hair, and with only a brief glance in the windshield of a

148

neighboring car, headed for the barbecue sandwiches. Later, on our way home, I yelled this into Ron's ear: "It's entirely possible that a very large percentage of the bad moods I've had in our thirty-year marriage are directly attributable to my hair."

Emancipation

*H*air is a big issue for women. I can't even count the times it's played a role in my decision making. Or the times I've planned out my perms and haircuts around the important events in my schedule.

For twenty-four years I've done the permanent wave thing—I remember because I had my first perm when I was pregnant with Matt. With my thin, straight hair, a legacy from my dear mother, I thought perms would be the only solution to my ever-present need for body. But they only gave me good hair about one-third of the time. The first month the curls were too tight, the last month, too loose.

When my longtime hairdresser took a three-week vacation just when I needed her, I took a chance on a new person and place. "Change me," I said.

"No more perm?" they asked, pleading. "Can we color your hair?"

"Okay," I said. And off it all came. I walked out many hours later with short hair and highlights.

Why did I wait so long, I've been asking myself. It sounds overdramatic, but, really, my whole life has changed. I'm saving countless hours a year. Not money—short hair means more frequent cuts and salon-applied hair color is not cheap—but time and, more important, emotion.

Come to think of it, cutting and coloring my hair may be more of an emancipation than having my children move out.

The Kids Are Gone,
the Dogs Are Dead

⌘

The kids are gone, the dogs are dead, and Ron and I are dating again. We're free to take off whenever we feel like it. There's a spontaneity about our lives that I don't think we've ever had, even in the six years we were married before our children were born.

This morning he says to me, "Let's go to Warner Ranch (a near-by rustic resort) for the night." I'm ambivalent—a little tired to think of packing, a little "dead-lined" to think of being away from my office and computer, a little guilty to think of missing church tomorrow morning. But we're trying to take times like these to go off on the spur of the moment, to do the unexpected, to run away.

So I agree, still ambivalent but willing, and throw in one pair of shorts and an extra shirt and my new favorite book, Annie Dillard's *An American Childhood*. Off we go, stopping at Fat Ivan's for a lunch of Caesar salad and all-you-can-eat ribs. Too much, too heavy, delicious. Ah well.

When we arrive at the Ranch we check into our tiny bungalow—no phone, no TV, but 100-watt bulbs in the lamps!—and head off to the golf course. *I* think we're looking for a TV to watch Tiger Woods in the U.S. Open, but Ron signs us up straightaway for the last tee time of the day. "First, dear," I say, "I have to hit a bucket of balls." I haven't played golf for nearly a year. And I'm terrible. After a while I'm proud to say I've played six holes and don't yet have a blister on my thumb, which means I'm beginning to hold my club right. It's 6:00 P.M. and we're nearly alone on the course, which is how I like it. No one but Ron is watching me tee off—or get teed off—and the times I miss the ball completely are fewer and farther between.

The course we're playing is surrounded by untended foothill shrubbery, wild flowers, and equally wild grasses. The contrast between the manicured fairways and the wildness of the rest of the countryside makes this evening even more wonderful. I love the juxtaposition of the tended and the untended, the tame and the wild. Inside, I feel just like this ground—manicured yet wildly out of control, a mix of culture and freedom, fitting in and individuality.

I love Warner Ranch because it feels welcoming and non-censorious. Everyone's in shorts and flip-flops; dressing for dinner requires a little decorum, but nothing fancy.

Pony Express riders and the Butterfield stage used to stop here in the 1800s; it was the halfway station between the Colorado River and the Pacific Ocean. Kit Carson lodged in one particular bungalow when he was "in town." Movie stars came for the restorative hot springs in the early 1900s: Clark Gable, Carol Lombard, Bing Crosby. Many of the old bungalows are still in service; the walls more than one-foot thick, smooth and rounded with stucco. The surrounding trees stand tall, leafy, and grand the way old trees should.

The hot springs, smelling sulfurous and capable of tarnishing my silver jewelry in a moment if I forget and wear it in the water, bubble out of the ground and are piped into the largest hot tub I've ever seen. At night we float under the stars, classical music playing soothingly from the speakers, muted laughter floating out of the steam.

This weekend the Ranch is nearly filled to capacity. School is recently out of session for the summer, and the grounds are filled with children—skinny little boys wearing trunks that hang to their kneecaps, tiny little girls with poochy tummies and bathing suits all colors of the rainbow. They run barefoot in the grass, tumbling over balls and pool toys. Several young boys, brown and smooth-skinned, are jumping on a plastic air bubble that in turn shoots a small rocket up through the tree branches. It works so well it catches all our attention. One little girl in polka dots dances to the live band set up on a portable stage. They're singing "Summertime," so appropriate because that's what it feels like, and summer begins officially in just a few days.

Ron and I are enjoying more barbecue, reveling in the sounds of the children, and (though we miss them dreadfully) glad that those sounds are not from our own kids. We love being here alone; we have a bit of chocolate cake and head off for the hot tub. It's 8:30 and still light.

I can't pinpoint exactly what it is that makes this twenty-four-hour getaway so important to me. Maybe it's the fact that, once I put aside my ambivalence, we both wanted to come to the same place at the same time. Maybe it's the juxtaposition of the tiny children against our aloneness—and the fact that we feel complete even though without our kids. (Come to think of it, this may be the first time we've come here without them.) Maybe it's the further confirmation that we enjoy being together enough that we can do it without packing our space with friends, who might otherwise have joined us.

Maybe it's simply that we thought of it, and then just did it.

Dating Again—An Empty-Nest Moment

*O*ver at Jennie's house, on top of her piano, is the most hilarious picture of screaming Jennie (her hair standing on end like Frankenstein's wife's, her eyes tightly shut, her mouth open and round like a posthole) and her smiling husband, Bob, nearing the bottom of the slide at Splash Mountain. They did the Disneyland thing again, not long ago. Though they took a couple of their younger kids along, this was the first time since they dated over twenty-five years ago (because their littlest could now go off with her big sister) that Mom and Dad were alone together in the park.

They make weekly dating a priority in their lives. But wandering around Disneyland alone? Jennie was severely nonplussed. Bob wanted to make out in the dark, for heaven's sake. He wanted *her* again, the old Jennie he'd fallen in love with in the first place. For a while, though, Jennie felt just plain sad. It took some adapting—the setting threw her—but after she adjusted, Jennie says, they had a blast.

I can relate to that bewildering feeling. Disneyland is a family affair. It doesn't seem right to be there without your children (even if they're merely over in Tomorrow-land). And when you've compiled years of Disneyland memories as a family, as we who live in Southern California have, doing without them is strange. And it's even a little sad.

Yet, maybe that's the place we have to begin when we're reconstructing a love relationship with our husbands—going to the old places with a new perspective, going to new places where it was hard to take our kids, and being intentional about setting aside specific time to get to know each another.

I think it's called dating.

We Are Who We Are

I am who I am—*that* I've figured out. My personality is not going to change that much, but will become ever more my own, quirky and full of the stuff that would make a psychologist want me for her couch. I know how my body's time clock likes to be set and what foods agree with me—and what foods I'm willing to eat that don't necessarily agree with me. I know what happens when I indulge in too much sleep, too much television, too many desserts, and I don't like it. And I'm finally mature enough to avoid activities, movies, foods, and schedules that disturb my equilibrium.

And my body will remain uniquely mine, spotted like a fever with liver spots and lumpy where mothers' bodies become lumpy. I've stopped wishing to have the same gifts and natural abilities as my friends, or the same shape as my tiny-and-trim kickboxing instructor, Michelle. Almost.

It's the simplicity of growing older. And it happens, really, most concretely, when the children are gone because it's a product of focus. No longer can we avoid taking a good look at ourselves. There's no one else to get in the way of the mirror.

In one of those "Quote-a-Day" calendars, this one from *Bartlett's Familiar Quotations,* I read this wonderful comment by Jean Cocteau: "Mirrors should reflect a little before throwing back images." Don't you wish that were the case? Wouldn't it encourage you if your mirror could explain each new wrinkle by lining it up with the life experience that caused it? Come to think of it, and I'm being quite serious here, how can I disparage my stretch marks if I connect them with the two who put them there?

What freedom there is in the thought that we are who we are and that's okay! That we're old enough, *finally,* to know what we like and don't like, what we're good at and not so good at doing, what body type is natural and right for us.

Recently these opening sentences in my local newspaper caught my attention: "Few people had ever seen Elsie Zala naked—and most of them were doctors. At seventy-three, she figured it would likely stay that way." Elsie is one of thirteen San Diego women who posed in the nude for a San Diego sculptor as her contribution to a touring exhibit called "The Changing Face of Women's Health." The project was created to answer the question, posed by a social worker/psychotherapist and two OB-GYNs (all women), "If there was one major thing we could change that would impact women's health positively in the next century, what would we take on?" Their answer, "We decided we wanted to tackle the obsession with one-dimensional beauty and the starvation imagery that consumes women" (*San Diego Union-Tribune,* Tuesday, April 25, 2000).

These thirteen gutsy models reflect various seasons of a woman's life and most body types out there. The sculptures are small, ten inches high, yet beautiful—bodies of mature women, some standing proud, one curled up like a baby, all bumpy and lumpy like the rest of us. Though I doubt I would ever be tempted to join a project like that one, nor encourage my friends to flaunt their naked bodies, I'm secretly proud (well, not so secretly) of their chutzpa. I love their self-confidence. Wouldn't it be wonderful if we, who are as troubled by our waistlines as the rest of the world, could overcome our obsession with "one-dimensional beauty"?

Kickboxing

Yes, kickboxing. It's my new aerobic activity, and though I don't *love* it, and though I have to make myself go each time, it is doing good things to my body.

I've read that the reason older people shuffle when they walk is because one or more of the three specific methods of balance they use is weak—hearing, sight, or leg muscles. Hearing can be helped with aids, sight with glasses, but leg muscles have no such practical way of improvement. That's one reason I'm going—to strengthen my leg muscles. Also, I'm going in order to get a greater sense of my body. Other than regular walking I don't have a lot of physical activity in my life. An occasional golf swing, perhaps. Now and then a breast stroke.

I'm also going to get some beginning training in self-defense, although my fellow students and I concluded that unless the music's playing and the beat is right, we have no chance of defending ourselves.

There seems to come a time in a woman's life—a man's too, I suppose—when there is no more room for excuses. No time left to put off the gym. And now, though my arms still swing in the breeze, I'm feeling stronger and more in control with what happens to my body. I almost wish Ron would sneak up on me so I could take a punch at him—because I really don't want an encounter with an *actual* criminal.

161

Is It Hot in Here,
or Is It Just Me?

Not long ago I had my first hot flash. At least I think that's what it was. I'm in the middle of that no-woman's-land so cleverly called *perimenopause*, such a new word my spell checker doesn't even recognize it. I do, however, like the way that word lumps all my complaints into one. Makes me sound a little more in my right mind. Although in my condition, would I know what my right mind was like if I saw it? It's a good thing my kids aren't around too often.

My good friend, Toni, had a "senior moment" for an hour one day. In her words:

> It was a leisurely Saturday morning. Paul asked me to go to the office and pick up our check to deposit it at the bank. Not a hard task. When I got to the office and opened it up, I went to turn off the alarm and suddenly my mind went blank. Well, you only have thirty seconds to get "unblank." I froze! All at once the alarm went off with

this mind-numbing, brain-piercing siren. As I was frantically pushing combinations of buttons, I quickly called home but could hardly hear Paul with the alarm going off. I envisioned the police coming to arrest me. The alarm would not quit. After what seemed like an eternity, it stopped. Paul called the company, and I didn't get hauled in. So I grabbed the check and off to the bank I went.

A tad frazzled, I got out of the van and shut the door and then stopped. I'd locked my keys in the car! *Oh well*, I thought, *I'll crawl under and get the hide-a-key when I come back.*

Now I was not only frazzled but also mad at myself. Entering the bank, I tried to do the deposit but had mis-added the figures and messed up the whole transaction. I could not think. There was a long line of toe-tapping people behind me! Finally, I handed it all to the teller and let her figure it out. I'm sure she thought I must have never been to a bank before. Now I was frazzled, mad, and feeling *really* dumb.

I left, crawled under the van and retrieved the spare key. Then I drove across the parking lot to fill up with gas. As I was filling up, I was trying to figure out exactly what had gone wrong at the bank. I became aware in my rear view mirror of someone waiting for my spot at the tank. No problem. I shut my door, put the car in gear, and pulled forward. One slight problem—I had forgotten to take the hose out of the car. I jerked the entire hose right out of pump #5 and saw it dangling from my gas tank. I gathered it up and humbly entered the station (which was filled with men only, of course). Need I tell you the looks I received? I meekly handed the hose to the attendant and apologized profusely under the stares and smirking smiles of all those men. The attendant shook his head, rolled his eyes, told me to forget it, and motioned for me to be on my way.

By now I was physically shaking. Driving home I began to cry, then laugh, then cry, then laugh. I just wanted to go back to bed where it was safe!

Of course the really funny thing is that we've all been there, in one circumstance or another, and can completely relate.

We joke about menopause and PMS and hormonal dysfunction until it hits us full in our flushed little faces. Age jokes *are* funny; don't we each have a mug or two sitting in our cupboards that is supposed to make us laugh? (From the Internet come the "Benefits of Growing Older": In a hostage situation you are likely to be released first, things you buy now won't wear out, your secrets are safe with your friends because they can't remember them either, your supply of brain cells is finally down to a manageable size, and so on.)

I thought this stage of my life would be a breeze, that I'd be prepared to be a middle-aged woman. After all, as my mother always said, "Middle age is ten years older than you are." With all that time I should have been ready.

But now that it's arrived, I'm not as blasé as I thought I'd be. I'm lathering on the hair color and tanning cream and watching the age spots collect on my arms and legs like mosquito bites in the jungle. And the words "risk," "adventure," and "daring" make me think about my bones.

Sometimes it's risky just getting up in the morning. Every day we have to deal with the uncertainty of life and with the emotions that assail us as we, consciously or unconsciously, compare ourselves to the more aggressive women out there. The younger ones. The smarter ones.

But age is in the mind. One of my best friends is Nancy, seventy-six years old, gray, and stooped. Last year she went on a missions trip to Ireland. In preparation, she spent a weekend in Tijuana, sleeping on the floor, learning how to find her way around in a foreign culture. A month before that, she took the train by herself from San Diego to the Colorado mountains for a family reunion. She's publishing articles on her recent widowhood, mentoring young women, and showing up at church whenever the doors open. She really prefers living alone.

Is Nancy a risk taker? You bet. She's risking her well-earned right to sit back and take it easy. While she's not rappelling down mountain faces, she's busy finding other ways to take herself out of her comfort zone.

Nancy is accustomed to adventure. She met her husband in Costa Rica where she managed a resort. He floated in on his boat with his wife, who died suddenly at the resort. After a while, he took Nancy with him as crew, and then as wife, and off they sailed. They lived on a boat in the San Diego harbor for years and years. Nancy says Lin's most oft-heard direction to her was, "We're taking a trip. Be ready in thirty minutes." It was a life of change and excitement that she absolutely loved.

Nancy is my model of an older woman, a woman content with her body, happy in her situation, missing her husband, but still ready for life. I want to *be* her. I'd love it if the Lord said, "Be ready in thirty minutes," and what He meant was, "Give Me thirty minutes and I'll make you like Nancy." But I don't think He works like that.

Beaches and Redwoods

꧂

$\mathcal{M}$y husband does everything fast, from brushing his teeth to rubbing my back to typing on his computer keyboard. And when he goes on vacation he wants to *get* there ASAP and plant for a while. That's why I've been mighty surprised to recognize and document his new appreciation for car travel. Maybe because it's just the two of us now, and we know each other so well—what we like to do and eat and visit—that he's even suggesting we make another car trip. Again with no agenda.

I am so delighted there are no words for it.

This time we meet up in Seattle at the airport and rent a car (they give us a minivan because the midsized car we paid for isn't available, and we don't mind at all). This trip we have thirteen days to travel the twelve hundred miles between Seattle and San Diego. Again, no reservations and very few plans. Several days with family near Seattle, a quick visit to Jesse, another to Molly. Lots of time by the Pacific, a few giant redwoods, the Golden Gate Bridge. Matt's in the Philippines, so we send him our non-plans by e-mail. He's slightly jealous, but having the time of his life.

It's hard to believe, but this time we both have our computers and our cell phones along. Ron reports that he gets 75-100 e-mails a day. I average only three or four. When I log on and find a full screen of messages I panic. I can't imagine how Ron would feel with thirteen days of e-mail piled up. He says to me that he's glad I'm part of the information age now and can understand his need to keep in touch.

∽

A management consultant once told me that many executive divorces are helped along by the growing disparity of business savvy between the husband and the-stay-at-home wife. He plans his professional growth and goals year by year and moves up the ladder, adding secretaries and employees. She, because she doesn't have to work, stays home with the kids, irons his shirts, cleans his house, prepares his meals. As she should. But after a while, he's moving in an entirely different level from where he began. Nothing has changed for her. She's still ironing, cleaning, and cooking as she's done for thirty years.

The point was not that wives should not be doing those things anymore, but that, without care, the gulf of sophistication between husband and wife can drive them farther apart.

Then this consultant said to me, "It's all right for you to hire help to clean your house. If you can find someone who will accomplish your goal eighty percent as well as you could do it yourself, for ten dollars an hour or less, it's a good deal."

So I hired a weekly housekeeper. What a terrific idea.

∽

The highlights of our trip were the beach days, two at Canon Beach on the Oregon Coast and two at Laguna Beach just a couple hours north of our home. We had spent many wonderful days at Canon Beach as a young couple. There is an old Christian conference center there where we came for many retreats, to hear great speakers on the Christian life, to walk the beach and pray, to revel in creation, to fall in love. It was there I learned that worshiping God can happen anywhere, anytime, and though connection with a local church is vital to a healthy spiritual walk, you don't have to wait until Sunday to commune with God. And occasionally you can even spend a Sunday at the beach. I loved that lesson.

Canon Beach was delightful. My favorite part was a limited hike in Ecola State Park—limited because I just couldn't get Ron to go *far* enough. Yet Ron—he's a beach boy—blesses me when he agrees to any kind of hiking in the woods. The trail began in the park and wound up and down and up again high above the ocean, then back once more under the trees. I'd brought along my hiking/walking shoes—cross-training gear at its most useful—and reveled in the dark path, speckled with leaves and sunlight. I love the Oregon woods. They are lush and green, overgrown, smelly with the good decay of vegetation. So unlike the Colorado forests of my childhood.

A few days later we drive into Laguna, another old haunt yet from a not-so-distant time. The crowds are greater, the available rooms rarer, the fare higher. But we find a perfect place where the sound of the waves is so loud it drowns out all but the most raucous around us. We shop a little, visit some art galleries, and take time to see the Pageant of the Masters, a magnificent and unbelievable live staging of great paintings and sculptures that astonishes us.

But the greatest part of those two days is the quiet mornings. Up early, coffee, walks, breakfast on a patio near our room that no one else at the hotel seems to have discovered. We decide that while we like doing some sight-seeing, and there are a few interesting shops to explore, our favorite activity on vacation is...nothing. Quiet. Leisurely meals. Beautiful surroundings. In that way, we are so much alike.

During our trip we visit relatives, one who has what appears to be early-onset Alzheimer's. One day, playing golf, is especially telling. She picks up my ball when she comes across it and must be told over and over which way we're going. Once, when she had but a two-foot putt left, she elected instead to stand between the pin and the ball and prepared to drive it off the green as if it were a tee-shot.

As I watch her husband's patient frustration—the four of us sit down to dinner that night with a salad she's made big enough for twelve—I think of Robertson McQuilken again. I begin to consider more carefully just what it is I've asked of Ron. One thing that occurs to me, albeit belatedly, is that when a loved one is desperately ill, it is not merely the caretaker whose life is disrupted—it's the entire family. I begin to acknowledge that deliberately requiring someone I love to commit to the agony of such a life is not the way to approach this at all. I'm a little ashamed that I've been so adamant, so insistent that Ron see things as I see them. And now I'm thinking that what I really want to say is don't let me tie you down, don't let me stay home when I get ill enough that you or our children or our grandchildren are uncomfortable.

Instead, get me in a good place!

I know I sound macabre, talking about death, dying, illness. I'm only fifty, for heaven's sake. But this is the time we begin considering such things, and I'm a planner. I tell Ron what I'm thinking, and why I'm thinking it. I'm not sure what's going on in his mind, but I feel I've let him off a bit of a hook. I hope I've let him know I trust him to care for me.

Reflecting

Been There,
Done That

*It's the first week of school, September 2000. The streets around my house and the nearby elementary school are clogged with SUVs and minivans, the sidewalks crowded with tiny bodies shouldering huge backpacks or, as is currently the rage, pulling the backpacks behind them.

I walk past moms standing at the school fence, watching their children on the playground. Frowns pucker their foreheads, tears puddle in their eyes. I know just how they feel and am torn between putting my arm around one or two of them and skipping by singing, *been there, done that.*

For some time now I haven't made the school supplies run, haven't had the fun of rounding up new pencils and paper, notebooks and lunch boxes. No scrounging the mall for back-to-school clothes, no last minute excitement as we walk into a classroom and meet a teacher for the first time, see who's in the class. No back-to-school night, no car pools, no September anxiety.

I *miss* all that stuff. In a way, it's a symbol of the passing of time, the markers that measure the growth of my family. It's been far and away the most satisfying business I've ever put my hand to, this parenting thing. And though part of me mourns its being over, if you think about it, I wonder if it ever really *is*.

Even today I begin my quiet time with a heavy heart. My children are wrestling with finances, with career choices, with life decisions, and there's just enough emotion floating around that I can't get away from it. In fact, it's been collecting over my head like a cloud, and though I know none of this is supposed to be *my* burden, I'm allowing it to follow me around. And I'm wanting to hover again.

As I read my Bible and devotional books and pray, I have the hardest time focusing in on anything but the situations immediately surrounding those I love. I go out for my walk (oh, what a beautiful morning!) and tell the Lord over and over what I want Him to do for my children—provide jobs, housing, cars, careers. I fully believe He wants me to tell Him everything I'm thinking and all that I want Him to do. He's promised to act on those prayers. Yet He often has additional things to say to me. I heard Him this morning, got this deep sense of understanding: *Mary*, He said to me, *you're asking Me to do things for your children that will keep them from having to work hard at something, that will keep them from learning, and maybe even keep them dependent on you.*

"Ah ha," I said back to Him. "I get it now…again. Once more I'm praying for things and comforts, while You're concerned with character. I know that, I knew that. Really, it's what I want, too."

A mother and her small boy walk past me. He's blond like Matt was at his age, looks deep in thought. I see angst on his face, and I wonder what he's thinking, or worrying, about. A bully? His spelling words? Not knowing *exactly* where to go or what to say or who to sit with? I long to get inside him, to be a small voice in his head, to tell him over and over, "You'll do fine! You're so smart! Everyone will like you!"

But that's not my job. This boy's mom will have to provide that voice. I've done my share, paid my dues, raised my kids. Yet, come to think of it, these are words I still need to say to my precious children as they finally go out on their own:

You'll do fine! You're so smart! Everyone will like you!

Endings

I've traveled a great distance, internally and emotionally, over the years represented in this book. I'm always surprised to look back and see progress in my life—sometimes I move so very slowly—but I know it's there. Frankly, I'm glad to have this record that I've grown from wanting to clutch my children to me for the rest of our lives to wanting them *out*.

Progress is God's intention for us. Moving ahead. Changing. Becoming. The destination is important, but it's the journey that readies us for our arrival.

I'm still learning lessons about letting go. Though it's not my inclination, I can't resist summing all this up, if only to give myself some tangible proof that God has been at work. Maybe something here will be of some help to you.

WHILE YOUR KIDS ARE STILL LIVING UNDER YOUR ROOF...

1. *Take every opportunity to create lasting memories and milk family traditions for all they're worth.*

Anything out of the ordinary—spontaneous celebrations, spontaneous eating out, spontaneous car trips—creates a memory. These are the happenings, the unique-to-our-family events that link us together.

Memories are also made through routine—popcorn for Monday night football, hamburgers on Saturdays, jigsaw puzzles over the holidays.

You may feel it is too late to create new traditions just as your children are leaving for what feels like forever. But take some time to think over the previous few years; sometimes just having particular food at a particular table or with particular dishes says "memory" to your child. Ask her about favorite meals, memories, activities, or choices that set your family off from others. What would she not want to miss when she's home for the holidays?

2. Look for opportunities to be together without other distractions.

Most of us can create some togetherness in a car at one time or another. Don't send your college student off to school on the train if you can spare the time to drive him there. Offer to ride along on trips to the airport or errands that take some significant travel time. There are few places better than cars for talk time—if you keep the music down.

The temptation may be to carry on with your "new" life. But though our kids don't want us hovering, they do want to know that we are still available to give them the time and counsel they need. And I think they want to know we're a little flummoxed by this new life of ours, the one without them around all the time.

3. *Allow them to make mistakes.*

Management expert Peter Drucker says the better a man is, the more mistakes he will make. Are you inclined (like I am) to so protect your children that they don't have mistakes to learn from, even when they're grown? If bad choices are part of the learning process toward making good choices, then what on earth are we doing?

This doesn't mean we should say nothing when we see our kids heading off in a really harmful direction. It means we bite our tongues when it comes to unnecessary advice, such as what to wear, hair color and style, or how to spend their money and their time. When our children are living at home, we're the most apt to intervene; yet what better place for them to do the experimentation and make the mistakes critical to healthy adulthood? We're past the stage of great influence in these choices; the time has come to *really* let natural consequences take over.

4. *Keep looking for those teachable moments.*

Could it be, now that moving out is drawing near, they're more ready to hear what you have to say and learn from you? Enlist their help in the maintenance of the house. Don't let them move out (like my kids did) without having fixed a toilet or changed a doorknob. Assign them meals to make, including the shopping; require them to keep their own checking account and pay their own bills. Charge them whatever you want for rent, food, just for the privilege of living in your home. (But be sensitive to their individual situations.)

5. Continue to hold your own values and house rules high. After all, they're still living under your roof. If they don't like it, they can move.

Giving your children growing room in your home doesn't mean you need to throw your standards out the window. More than ever, our kids need to see us holding strong to what we've always taught them. It's another level of pressure to live that way with adult kids at home. They're much more aware of the impact of these values in their own lives now and are most likely doing the final evaluation of our faith and lifestyle, trying them on for size, if you will. Just because they're bigger than we are, can argue more fluently, and stay up later—and have youth on their side—doesn't mean who and what we are and say is not still vitally important to their development.

6. Resist the urge to hover over older children. It is never helpful.

When we hover over our grown kids, even our nearly grown kids, we send a message to them of uncertainty. "You can't really do this on your own. I don't trust you to follow through, to make the right choice, to make this contact in the right manner." Can you imagine if you set your young adult up in a job or an opportunity and he or she could not handle it?

Every now and then it is appropriate to link arms with our kids to help them along. But as a general rule, let them initiate their own contacts, follow up and through on their own ideas. Give advice when you're asked and not before, or at least ask permission. Be an advisor, not an authority.

7. Welcome criticism!

If you haven't yet learned how to "take it" from your children, do so at your first opportunity. Give and take on critical issues is what makes for mature relationships. The best way to grow as a person, the best way to encourage growth in others, the best way to nurture an adult relationship, is to make yourself vulnerable. This is the living out of "bear one another's burdens" from Galatians 6, which, in the context, applies to weakness of character.

Ask your children to point out areas in your life that need adjustments. Be specific. Enquire, "What would you like me to change in the way I relate to you?" Enlist their help as partners in growth. In time they will give you the same privilege. And by then that's exactly what it will feel like—a privilege rather than a right, responsibility, or...revenge.

WHEN THEY BEGIN THE PROCESS OF MOVING OUT...

1. Recognize that independence has been your goal all along.

Signs of independence—handling finances and laundry, making new friends, *not* calling home—are what we should be looking and rooting for, not cringing over. So many of us mothers want our kids independent in theory, but when it comes down to "me or them" we actually have our *own* best interests at heart.

Remind them that independence carries its own responsibility. My kids don't have a curfew when they're home, but I ask them for their estimated time of arrival. I expect them to let me know if they will be much later so I won't worry. It's a matter of respect, this time, not hovering.

2. *Encourage your kids to leap out of their comfort zones.*

In many cases, our reluctance to encourage our kids to try new things or go new places is what holds them back in the first place, whether from an unwillingness to worry us, or respect for our feelings, or simply an identification with our fear. But none of us want our kids to be fearful.

Encouragement is the tool we use to push our birdlets out of the nest. Youth has a built-in daring; all it needs is our approval and that tiny nudge of enthusiasm. I am *thrilled* that both my children love roller coasters even though I've never been on one with them and don't like to even think of what they've ridden!

3. *Learn to embrace your* child's *dreams for his life, not* your *dreams for his life.*

That may be one of our hardest lessons. It's no problem if their dreams turn out to be grander than ours; but if they're not, or are radically different, it can become an issue. There is no greater confirmation we can give our children than to encourage their own dreams to grow. And to have the patience and love to wait out the growing.

4. *Recognize that your son's or daughter's new "home" is part of the launching.*

Molly's transference of small talk from me to her roommates demonstrated her comfort not only in her new relationships but also with me. I would hate to think that she might feel guilty for sharing more with her friends. It's a sign of a healthy relationship that a mom can let go of some of the confidences she's accustomed to holding.

It will also prepare you for sharing your adult child with a spouse. Practice untying the apron strings. Amazingly, the more willing we are to let loose, the sooner they check in.

WHEN THEY'RE GONE AND THE INEVITABLE HAS FINALLY HAPPENED…

1. *Evaluate your perspective.*

An empty nest is a prime opportunity for depression, or if not that, for a serious bout of self-pity. But this is a natural stage of life, for our kids and for us, and we can deal with it! When we have our perspective right, a perspective that includes all the good years we've had together, it's much easier to suppress the emotions until the kids are out of sight. Then a good cry is very appropriate!

2. *Branch out and try something new.*

Seriously, and I speak from experience, there is never an easy time for women like me to change. But life without change is slow death. We know that in our heads. And now we have time and the opportunity to cheat that slow death by gathering up our skirts—or tying our running shoes—and getting out there!

3. *Acknowledge your regrets, but don't wallow in them.*

None of us is perfect. That is an idea we must get over! There may be a place for a needed apology to our kids, but in most cases what's done is done.

Sometimes empty-nest time means it's time to give up—not on our kids, but on how much we let their choices affect our happiness. It's time to give up the guilt, the hurt, the worry. God wants us to relate to Him as He's told us to—to trust Him, to pray, to put away the sin of worry, even the guilt we may feel. That's what He died for, to take away the worry and guilt, to forgive us for all those weaknesses. He also died for our children and ultimately will hold them accountable for their choices as adults. It's up to them now.

4. Look back in thankfulness.

If you're a parent, you have just finished, for the most part, the most significant job God will ever give you to do. Pick out the wonderful memories and let go of the rest.

When you put your focus on thankfulness, on all the good years together, on the emerging of what you were working on—a responsible, healthy adult—there can be no other response. When what you were working on is still a promise but not yet a reality, God works through our thankful hearts and wants our continued trust regardless of the circumstances.

5. Keep praying!

Never before have we been so out of the loop, so out of control, of our children's lives. We need to learn to pray with the fervency of a warrior, fighting for the safety and strength of character of our children. No more can we sneak into their bedrooms and check on them; rarely can we feel their foreheads for fever. But, as was always the case, God is there, waiting for us to ask His presence and intervention—and comfort.

Every morning I claim the promises and protection of Psalm 91. I picture each family member, including the up-coming ones, and ask God for physical protection (from accidents, attacks, illness), for spiritual protection (from believing the lies Satan throws at us), for relational and emotional protection (particularly for the new couple), for mental and intellectual protection (that we would be able to focus on the jobs the Lord has called us to).

This is hovering at its best, at its most effective.

6. *Concentrate on that man you married, who still lives in that nest you're calling empty!*

Now that the distractions are gone, focus, focus, focus! How fun it will be to rediscover each other again! In most marriages, it will be the wife who does the pursuing this time, who recognizes the importance of working on the marriage and the value of nurturing her husband. We seem to feel the distance first. And we have such power to begin the rejuvenation process. Our attitude, our energy, our bucking of the status quo, is what will revitalize our marriages.

Epilogue

*N*ests seem to empty in stages, as well they should. I look at it as part of the graciousness of God that, so far at least, I haven't had to handle the aloneness all at once. Just when I think they're both gone forever someone calls: *I'm coming home.*

Matt called, in fact. Though I sent him off tearfully, prepared for a year's separation (at least), work has evolved to the place where coming home to California serves the purpose best. He's been gone four months.

Molly and Jesse are here, having postponed their wedding for a season. Best laid plans of mice and mothers. Ah, well. I'm proud of them. The bridal shop is storing the dress, the busy bridesmaids sigh with relief that their holidays will be less stressful. I wonder what I'll do with this extra time.

Thankfully, once more my house is full of people who like each other. I just pulled two loaves of banana bread from the oven. The refrigerator is stocked and the shelves are bulging with food my kids like and, though I hate to cook, with them home it is a sweet sacrifice to do so. Their recently clean, neat bedrooms are filled again with all their wordly goods and music is pouring out of their doors. The phone's ringing like before, and once more we're having to juggle the cars.

I know it won't last. And you know what? *I don't want it to!* I'm finally ready for the break, the moving on that promises to clean out our garage and move all the boxes of kid stuff to new homes. Theirs.

I'm ready to travel with Ron, or to stay home by myself when I must. I'm ready to ride his scooter with him to the store, or a high school football game, or out to dinner when we feel like it. I'm ready to pare down and clean out, and to plant a new crop of flowers now that fall is here. I'm ready to put the finishing touches on this book, which is a struggle now, because there's so much going on!

Really, a nest never needs to be empty, if you define it as an emotional, loving connecting place where your family and others are welcome to come and go. It's that coming and going, that open door, those loving arms that make a family continue its commitment to one another. If the *hearts* are full, the empty rooms aren't so intimidating; and when those empty rooms *do* get to you, there are plenty of people out there who'd like your attention.

And there's always grandchildren. My friends tell me they're even better.

Other Good
Harvest House Reading

The Power of a Praying™ Wife
by Stormie Omartian
Every woman who desires a closer relationship with her husband will appreciate this refreshing look at the power of prayer in marriage. Along with real-life illustrations, Stormie also includes sample prayers and "power tools"—verses that inspire and encourage—to help wives rest in the assurance of God's wonderful promises of restoration, renewal, and growth in marriage.

The Power of a Praying™ Parent
by Stormie Omartian
Award-winning singer and songwriter Stormie Omartian and her husband, Michael, have spent the past 20 years raising their children...and learning the power of praying for them. Now, in 30 short, easy-to-read chapters, she shares how you can pray through every age and stage of your child's life.

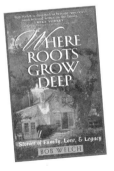

Where Roots Grow Deep
by Bob Welch
This spiritually satisfying collection of stories celebrates the bond of family and the enduring value of leaving a legacy of caring and character. Here you'll discover the richness of your own life and faith and lasting treasures to be handed down with love.

Living the Questions
by Carolyn Arends

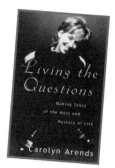

Carolyn Arends, whose music has been acclaimed for its artistry and lyrical power, offers us a very special glimpse into "the cruel, short, beautiful, long adventure that is this life." In her humorous, tender, and passionate collection of personal stories, Carolyn examines many of the struggles we face in light of her belief that God guides each of us safely through the mess and mystery of life. *Living the Questions,* while resisting easy solutions, suggests that our questions themselves tell us much about a final Answer almost too wonderful to imagine.

The Best Is Yet to Come
by Ann Platz

It's time for a middle-age celebration! Author and renowned interior designer Ann Platz shares the refreshing news that life after 40 is only the beginning. As a woman coming into the full knowledge of God's unlimited love, vast compassion, and comforting truths, you are entering a season of joyful productivity, profound clarity, and newness of vision.